UNDERSTANDING Z

Cambridge Tracts in Theoretical Computer Science

Titles in the series

1. G. J. Chaitin *Algorithmic Information Theory*
2. L. C. Paulson *Logic and Computation*
3. J. M. Spivey *Understanding Z*
4. G. E. Revesz *Lambda-Calculus, Combinators and Functional Programming*

UNDERSTANDING Z

A specification language and its formal semantics

J. M. SPIVEY
Oriel College, Oxford

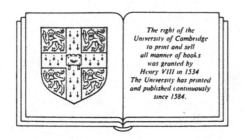

The right of the
University of Cambridge
to print and sell
all manner of books
was granted by
Henry VIII in 1534
The University has printed
and published continuously
since 1584.

CAMBRIDGE UNIVERSITY PRESS

Cambridge

New York   Port Chester

Melbourne   Sydney

CAMBRIDGE UNIVERSITY PRESS
Cambridge, New York, Melbourne, Madrid, Cape Town, Singapore, São Paulo

Cambridge University Press
The Edinburgh Building, Cambridge CB2 8RU, UK

Published in the United States of America by Cambridge University Press, New York

www.cambridge.org
Information on this title: www.cambridge.org/9780521334297

First published 1988
Reprinted 1992
This digitally printed version 2008

A catalogue record for this publication is available from the British Library

Library of Congress Cataloguing in Publication data
Spivey, J.M.
Understanding Z
(Cambridge tracts in theoretical computer science)
Bibliography: p.
Includes index.
1. Z (Computer program language) 2. Programming
languages (Electronic computers – Semantics). I. Title
II. Series.
QA76.73.ZS65 1988   005.13′3   87-33841

ISBN 978-0-521-33429-7 hardback
ISBN 978-0-521-05414-0 paperback

CONTENTS

Preface   vii

1 Introduction   1
    1.1. Introducing Z   2
    1.2. Why formal semantics?   7
    1.3. Meta-circularity   9
    1.4. Z and other methods   10
    1.5. Overview   16

2 Basic Concepts   18
    2.1. The world of sets   18
    2.2. Types   25
    2.3. Signatures, structures, and varieties   30
    2.4. Notation for denotational semantics   36
    2.5. The language of schemas   42

3 The Semantics of Z   46
    3.1. Language summary   47
    3.2. Modelling scope   51
    3.3. Declarations   56
    3.4. Terms   59
    3.5. Predicates   70
    3.6. Schema bodies   72
    3.7. Schema designators   72
    3.8. Schema expressions   78
    3.9. Specifications   81

4 Discussion   83
   4.1. Generic definitions   83
   4.2. Referential transparency   89
   4.3. Partially defined terms   90
   4.4. Z and Clear   93
5 Studies in Z Style   98
   5.1. Reasoning about specifications   98
   5.2. Specifying basic types   106
   5.3. Specifications and programs   111
   5.4. Why non-determinism is needed   114
   References   119
   Summary of Notation   123
   Index of Definitions   130

PREFACE

The Z notation is a language and a style for expressing formal specifications of computing systems. It is based on a typed set theory, and the notion of a "schema" is one of its key features. A schema consists of a collection of named objects with a relationship specified by some axioms, and Z provides notations for defining schemas and later combining them in various ways, so that large specifications can be built up in stages. Schemas can have generic parameters, and there are operations in Z for creating instances of generic schemas.

This book is about the mathematical background of Z. Its main aim is to give a formal semantics for Z, by which the meaning of constructs in the notation is described using concepts from mathematical logic. Such a formal semantics justifies the claim that Z is a precise specification language, and provides a standard framework for understanding specifications. After an introduction comparing Z and other specification methods, the main part of the book begins with the construction of *semantic domains* for Z—spaces of values in which the meaning of specifications lie. Next, a denotational semantics for Z is given by defining semantic functions which link an abstract syntax with operations on the semantic domains. A discussion follows of some issues in the design of Z which are illuminated by the semantics. Finally, the theory of specification which underlies the semantics is applied to a number of studies in specification style, showing that Z can be used for a wide variety of specification tasks.

The book is not intended as an introduction to formal specification in general or to the Z method in particular; the expected audience is those who already have some knowledge of Z, and wish to deepen their understanding of the mathematical background of the method. I hope it will also be useful to those who wish to implement software tools to help with the construction and manipulation of Z specifications, by providing a concise description of the notation, in the context of which fine details of interpretation can be discussed. This is not a standard for the Z notation, but I hope that the mathematical techniques applied will be a useful tool in the standardization process.

This research was supported in part by a Research Studentship from the Science and Engineering Research Council of Great Britain. It could not have been carried out without the active help and encouragement of my colleagues at the Programming Research Group, and it is therefore my duty to thank them here. But what might have been a mere duty has been made a pleasure by the congenial atmosphere of the group under Tony Hoare's direction. My supervisor, Joe Stoy, has been a vital source of encouragement. Bernard Sufrin and Carroll Morgan have patiently watched the work taking shape during many long discussions, sometimes puzzling, sometimes controversial, but always productive, and it is with gratitude that I record my debt to them. Rod Burstall, my external D.Phil. examiner, made many illuminating suggestions. Lastly, my deepest gratitude is due to my wife Petronella, who provided moral support and culinary diversions, and finally rescued me from bed-sitters for good.

Oriel College, Oxford   J. M. S.
October, 1987

CHAPTER ONE

INTRODUCTION

The problems of producing reliable software quickly and economically have been widely discussed in recent years, and initial experience has indicated that the use of mathematical methods of specifying and designing software can contribute towards a solution. For these mathematical methods to become effective in industrial practice, certain prerequisites must be satisfied. First, the notations used to express specifications and designs must be standardized, so that workers on a large project can collaborate without misunderstanding, and so that text-books and training courses can be written. Second, software tools will be needed to assist with the storage and organization of specifications and designs, and to automate the manipulation of mathematical text. Both these prerequisites demand that the mathematical notation be stable and well-understood.

The style of software specification and design known as Z has had a long period of development, which has for the most part been characterized not by stability of notation but by its very opposite. The Z style has developed as a result of tackling practical examples and adapting the notation to their needs, and this has resulted in a style and a notation which are suitable for the specification of sizeable software systems. As the method has become mature, the need for radical changes in style and notation has lessened; development of Z is now at a stage when a standard notation can be fixed. As noted above, this will help to satisfy the needs of industry, as well as the needs of further research into specification-processing tools.

According to the principle of using mathematics to document specifications and designs, this means that we should try to describe the Z notation itself in a mathematical way. The central contention of this book is that such a mathematical description—a formal semantics of Z—is both feasible and beneficial. Before turning to an account of the formal semantics of Z, we pause to review its main features, to consider the nature of formal semantics, and briefly to compare Z with some other specification languages.

1.1   Introducing Z

This is not the place for a detailed tutorial on the Z notation and method, but a short example may be a useful reminder of the style of specification they encourage. The example is a small database recording people's names and their telephone numbers.

Several features of Z are illustrated by the example. First among these is the use of *schemas* to record both static aspects of the database system— what states it can occupy—and dynamic aspects—what events are possible in the life of the system. The use of schemas allows the specification to be presented gradually, with a close correspondence between the mathematical text and prose commentary. This makes it easy to explain the mathematics as it is presented and to relate the variables in the mathematical text to the system they describe. The operation of the database with correct input will be described first, then the *schema calculus* will be used to extend the specification to deal with errors in the input.

1.1.1   *Example: a small database*

The database contains a number of people's names, and against each name is stored a telephone number. It has operations for adding a new name and telephone number, and for enquiring what number is stored against a given name. The *state-space* of the database system is described by a schema called *PhoneDB*:

PhoneDB

$known : \mathbf{P}\ NAME$

$phone : NAME \nrightarrow PHONE$

$known = \mathrm{dom}\ phone$

Two *observations* of the state are introduced as components of this schema: the set *known* of names known to the database, and the partial function *phone* which records a telephone number against certain names. An *invariant* relationship between these observations is documented: that the names known to the database are exactly those for which a number is recorded. As an example, the following is a possible state of the system:

$$known = \{ \text{Smith}, \text{Jones}, \text{Robinson} \}$$

$$phone = \{ \text{Smith} \quad \mapsto 01\text{--}325\text{--}4939,$$
$$\qquad\qquad \text{Jones} \quad \mapsto 0865\text{--}54141,$$
$$\qquad\qquad \text{Robinson} \mapsto 0865\text{--}54141 \}$$

Even simple mathematics like this allows a degree of exactness in specification which is not easy to achieve with ordinary prose. For example, we have specified precisely that each person can only have one number, and that two people may share a number, as Jones and Robinson do in the example state. We have also avoided undesirable implications in specifying the state-space: there is no implied limit on the number of entries, nor is there an implied order in which they are stored. It has also been possible to describe the state-space without making a premature decision about the format of names and numbers.

Having described the state-space of the database, we can begin to describe the events which can happen. One such event is the addition of a new number to the database, and we describe it with a schema:

AddPhone _____

$\Delta PhoneDB$

$name? : NAME$

$number? : PHONE$

$name \notin known$

$phone' = phone \cup \{name? \mapsto number?\}$

This schema describes a state change from the state with observations *known* and *phone* to the one with observations *known'* and *phone'*; the declaration $\Delta PhoneDB$ introduces these four components of the schema. There are two inputs: *name?*, the new name to be added to the database, and *number?*, the number to be recorded against that name. By convention, these inputs are given identifiers which end in a question mark. The schema documents a pre-condition for the event to be successful: the new name must not already be one of those known to the database. It also gives the relationship which must hold between the state before the event and the state after it: the record of telephone numbers is extended with the new number.

If the *AddPhone* operation is activated with an input which does not satisfy the pre-condition, the specification says nothing about what happens:

the system may break. This means that the system is not very robust: it is easy to break it by trying to add a name twice. The task of understanding the specification is made easier, however, by initially ignoring the possibility that incorrect input will break the system. In the next subsection, we will extend the specification given here to make it robust.

From this specification of the *AddPhone* operation we can prove a simple theorem about how the set of names known to the database changes. As we expect, this set expands to include the new name:

$$known' = known \cup \{name?\}.$$

We prove this as follows, using the invariants on the states before and after the event:

$known'$

$$
\begin{array}{lr}
= \operatorname{dom} phone' & \text{[Invariant after]} \\
= \operatorname{dom}(phone \cup \{name? \mapsto number?\}) & \text{[Spec. of } AddPhone] \\
= (\operatorname{dom} phone) \cup \{name?\} & \text{[Facts about dom]} \\
= known \cup \{name?\}. & \text{[Invariant before]}
\end{array}
$$

Stating and proving properties like this one is an important way of increasing confidence that the specification is accurate.

Another event is the operation of finding a number in the database. Again we describe it with a schema:

```
┌─ FindPhone ─────────────────────────────
│ ΔPhoneDB
│ name? : NAME
│ number! : PHONE
├─────────────────────────────────────────
│ name? ∈ known
│ number! = phone(name?)
│ phone' = phone
└─────────────────────────────────────────
```

This operation has one input *name?*, the name to be looked up, and one output *number!*, the number recorded for that name; by convention, outputs have identifiers ending in an exclamation mark. The pre-condition of this operation is that the name be known to the database. The output of the operation is the corresponding telephone number, and the state of the database is unchanged by the operation.

To complete the specification, we describe the state occupied by the database when it is first brought in to use. In this initial state, no numbers are recorded:

```
┌─ Init ─────────────────────────────────
│ PhoneDB
├─────────────────────────────────────────
│ known = ∅
└─────────────────────────────────────────
```

1.1.2 *Handling errors*

The specification so far describes a simple database of names and telephone numbers. But this database is not robust, because incorrect input could cause it to break. The *schema calculus* can be used to extend the specification to say how errors in the input are to be handled.

We begin by describing a number of new events for the database. The pre-condition of each event describes circumstances under which one of the operations on the database may fail, and the post-condition specifies that the state of the system is unchanged. Each event has a shape described by the schema $\Xi PhoneDB$:

```
┌─ ΞPhoneDB ─────────────────────────────
│ ΔPhoneDB
├─────────────────────────────────────────
│ phone' = phone
└─────────────────────────────────────────
```

Each of the events will have an output *report!* for an error message, so the event corresponding to an *AddPhone* operation for a number already known might look like this:

```
┌─ AlreadyKnown ─────────────────────────
│ ΞPhoneDB
│ name? : NAME
│ report! : MESSAGE
├─────────────────────────────────────────
│ name? ∈ known
│ report! = 'Name already known'
└─────────────────────────────────────────
```

The output *report!* is of type *MESSAGE*, and we assume for the sake of the example that it is a character string.

There is also a schema describing the message which acknowledges a successful operation:

$\begin{array}{|l}
\hline
_Ok_____ \\
report! : MESSAGE \\
\hline
report! = \text{'Ok'} \\
\hline
\end{array}$

Now we can describe a robust version of the AddPhone operation as follows:

$$RAddPhone \;\hat{=}\; (AddPhone \wedge Ok) \vee AlreadyKnown.$$

Here the three schemas *AddPhone*, *Ok*, and *AlreadyKnown* are put together with the logical operators $\wedge$ and $\vee$ to give a new schema *RAddPhone*. This schema describes an operation which, whenever possible, behaves like *AddPhone* and gives the report 'Ok'; but if the name given is already known, it leaves the state of the database unchanged and issues an error report.

Similarly, for *FindPhone*, we can describe the conditions under which it is appropriate to issue the message 'Name not known':

$\begin{array}{|l}
\hline
_NotKnown_____ \\
\Xi PhoneDB \\
name? : NAME \\
report! : MESSAGE \\
\hline
name? \notin known \\
report! = \text{'Name not known'} \\
\hline
\end{array}$

Combining this with the previous specification of *FindPhone* gives a robust operation:

$$RFindPhone \;\hat{=}\; (FindPhone \wedge Ok) \vee NotKnown.$$

The two robust operations have been specified by putting together separate fragments of specification corresponding to normal operation and error handling. Sometimes it possible to implement operations in a way that reflects this separation, but often it is necessary to structure the implementation in a different way; the practicalities of implementation should not, however, dictate the structure of the specification, which should be designed for maximum clarity.

These are the chief features of the Z style of specification. Schemas are used to describe all aspects of the system under discussion: the states it can occupy, the transitions it can make from one state to another, and even, as we transform the specification into a design for an implementation, the relationship between one view of the state and another. Schemas may be combined in the schema calculus to build descriptions of complex entities from descriptions of their components. This allows a complex state-space to be broken into manageable pieces, and makes it possible to describe separately different aspects of a system's behaviour.

1.2 Why formal semantics?

A guiding principle of the Z approach to specification has been the use of the ordinary structures of mathematics in the writing of software specifications. There are several advantages in this: the familiar language of sets and relations proves to be sufficient to describe succinctly the abstract structures needed in programming, and is already known to every mathematician and also to many non-specialists. In following ordinary mathematical practice, we may notice that mathematicians—at least those who call themselves applied mathematicians—spend little time worrying about the 'formal semantics' of the notations they use and the 'rules of inference' used to manipulate them. Why should we be concerned with these things when we try to apply mathematics to the new sphere of software design?

A first answer lies on the nature of the notations themselves. The ordinary mathematician can regard his notation mainly as a system of abbreviations, so that the parts of a text written in mathematical notation are not different in kind from the parts written in English, at least as far as *content* is concerned. Of course, the *form* of mathematical notation suits it for purposes for which plain English text would be highly unsuited: the compactness and regularity of formulae make them easy to manipulate algebraically in a way that English text is not. But in their content, mathematical formulae can finally be regarded as abbreviations for—admittedly very lengthy—English sentences, and by carefully introducing his notations one by one, the mathematician can maintain his confidence that they are free from ambiguity. Connected with this character of mathematical notation as a system of abbreviations is the way in which the constant symbols in a formula refer to abstract mathematical objects, almost in the same way that proper names refer to people, streets and cities.

When we begin to construct mathematical descriptions of software, it soon becomes plain that one of the main difficulties lies in the sheer size of the descriptions which result. For this reason, it becomes necessary to introduce explicit means for giving structure to the description by naming parts of it, and referring to these named parts from other parts of the description, where they may be combined and extended in various ways.

The conceptual power of these notations for modularizing specifications should come as no surprise, for the importance of modularity is one of the clearest conclusions to emerge from experience with programming languages such as MODULA (Wirth, 1977). It is important to notice the difference between these notations for modularity and those introduced in the course of ordinary mathematical practice. In mathematical discourse, the names which are introduced refer directly to the mathematical objects under study. Here, the names refer instead to parts of the description itself: a schema is a piece of mathematical text, and its name refers to this text, rather than to any mathematical object. The structuring notations describe ways of combining and extending these fragments of text, rather than abbreviating direct constructions on mathematical objects.

So these specification-structuring facilities represent a deviation from, or rather an extension of, the ordinary practice of mathematics, and they need some explanation. It is this explanation which the formal semantics provides, beginning with a mathematical model for the content of a fragment of specification.

A second argument in favour of formal semantics is its consequences for the practice of specification. A formal semantics provides a foundation for a logical calculus for reasoning about specifications and deriving consequences from them. Deriving consequences from a specification is an important aid in checking that a specification captures correctly a customer's requirements, and in validating proposed implementations. Formal semantics also provides a view of specifications which abstracts from inessential details of syntax and presentation, and this view makes it possible to compare specification techniques in an objective way, and to investigate new specification language constructs.

Finally, the successful application of formal methods in industry will be helped by software tools for storing, editing, checking, and manipulating specifications. These software tools, if they are to be effective, must be designed in the same rigorous way as any other program, and this means starting from a formal specification. Part of this specification must be a description of the specification language to be supported. For some tools, such as specification editors, a formalized syntax of the specification language will be sufficient, but other tools, such as type-checkers, and, more particularly, any tools which assist with the construction of proofs about specifications, will need to depend on a formal semantics.

1.3 Meta-circularity

The formal semantics of the Z notation given in this book is itself written using Z as a meta-language. This idea of using a notation to give a 'meta-circular' description of its own semantics forms a long-standing tradition in Computer Science, beginning with McCarthy's definition of LISP (McCarthy, 1962) by means of an interpreter itself written in LISP. But the technique is open to the criticism that it doesn't really define anything. In informal terms, if someone didn't understand Z at all, we could hardly expect his understanding to be improved by a look at a formal semantics written in Z, although perhaps if he had a partial understanding, he could use the semantics to clear up some remaining areas of doubt. More formally, we might hope that the desired semantics might be found as a 'fixed-point' of the definition, but as Stoy (1977) points out, the least fixed point is bound to be 'bottom', the semantics in which every text is meaningless.

A more subtle problem is that two slightly different but inconsistent suppositions about the semantics can both be supported by a meta-circular definition. For example, unless special precautions are taken, a meta-circular definition of a programming language will not tell us whether parameters to subroutines are passed by name or by value. If we read the text of the definition under the assumption that parameters are passed by name, then the definition will appear to describe call-by-name, and if we assume call-by-value semantics, then the definition will appear to describe call-by-value: compare (Reynolds, 1972).

Why do these criticisms not invalidate a meta-circular definition of Z? One way of answering them would be to point out that the semantics consists simply of the development of a certain mathematical theory, and this development could, at least in principle, be carried out without using Z, but rather, say, the basic language of first-order logic. Indeed, we might hope that such a development of the theory would follow very closely the development given here using Z; this hope is encouraged by the fact that potentially problematic Z constructs such as generic schemas and the combining operators of the schema-calculus are avoided in our semantic meta-language, so that the description differs from an entirely first-order description mainly in the richness of the mathematical notation used.

This argument encourages us to see the meta-circular semantics ultimately as an informal sketch of a semantics which might be formalized fully in some more primitive but less expressive logical language. But in encouraging this view it seems to miss the point, because our aims in giving the semantics are rather different from those of logicians who seek a formal foundation for mathematics. Our purpose is not to give a grand consistency proof for the entire mathematical enterprise, nor to reduce mathematics to the most elementary terms possible, but rather to give a mathematical model which helps us to understand Z specifications and to reason about them, and this purpose is served just as well by a semantics expressed in Z as it would be by one expressed in more elementary terms.

What is more, if we are to use the formal semantics as part of the specification of software tools to assist with the process of writing and refining specifications, it is appropriate that the definition be already written in a notation designed for expressing software specifications. Writing the semantic definition in Z also provides a useful example of the flexibility of Z as a framework for developing mathematical theories.

1.4   Z and other methods

A number of different styles of mathematical specification are gaining popularity, and it is worth comparing Z with some of these. Broadly speaking, the styles are divided into *model-oriented* methods, where the aim of a specification is to construct an abstract model of the information system being specified, and *property-oriented* or *algebraic* methods, where the aim is to describe a system in terms of its desired properties, without constructing an explicit model. Among the model-oriented methods are Z and VDM (Jones, 1978, 1980, 1986; Bjørner & Jones, 1982); prominent algebraic methods are Clear (Burstall & Goguen, 1980, 1981; Sannella 1981, 1982), OBJ (Goguen, Thatcher & Wagner, 1978; Goguen & Tardo, 1979) and ACT ONE (Ehrig, Fey & Hansen, 1983).

This distinction between model-oriented and property-oriented methods is not as clear-cut as it might at first appear; in practice, Z specifications often describe certain aspects of systems by giving axioms which must be satisfied by the system, and this amounts to a property-oriented specification. Algebraic specifications often describe a collection of basic data-types in a property-oriented way, then use these to build a model of the system being specified.

1.4.1   *VDM*

The closest method to Z is the 'Vienna Development Method' (VDM), which originated at the IBM Vienna Laboratory, and has been developed in the work of Dines Bjørner and Cliff Jones. In their aims, VDM and Z are quite similar, but there are a number of differences of style which give each method its own advantages and disadvantages.

As an aid to comparison, what follows is a specification in the language of VDM of the telephone-number database from subsection 1.1.1. The state of the system is described in VDM as follows:

$$PhoneDB :: known : \textbf{set of } NAME$$
$$phone : \textbf{map } NAME \textbf{ to } PHONE$$
where
$$inv\text{-}PhoneDB \;\hat{=}\; known = \textbf{dom } phone.$$

As in Z, the two components of the state are introduced and given types, and an invariant relation between them is documented. The style of VDM discourages redundant state components, so the component *known* would probably be omitted here, since it can be derived from *phone* according to the invariant.

The operation of adding a new number might be specified like this:

$$AddPhone(name : NAME, number : PHONE)$$
$$\textbf{ext wr } known : \textbf{set of } NAME$$
$$\textbf{wr } phone : \textbf{map } NAME \textbf{ to } PHONE$$
$$\textbf{pre } name \notin known$$
$$\textbf{post } known = \overleftarrow{known} \cup name \wedge$$
$$phone = \overleftarrow{phone} \cup \{name \mapsto number\}.$$

The state components relevant to the operation are listed with their types in the **ext** clause, and they are marked as writable (**wr**). The pre-condition for the success of the operation and the post-condition established by its completion are documented as in Z, but they are separated. In the post-condition, the values of state-components in the initial state are denoted by decorating their names with a hook (e.g. $\overleftarrow{known}$).

The invariant on the final state is not an implicit part of the post-condition as it is in Z, so it is necessary to specify the final values of even derived state components such as *known*. This can make VDM specifications less concise than comparable Z specifications, and discourages the use of derived components, but it introduces a useful redundancy into the specification. Because the pre- and post-conditions are separated, it is possible to formulate *proof-obligations* on the writer of the specification: for the specification to be well-formed, the pre-condition must guarantee the existence of a final state satisfying the post-condition, and all such final states must satisfy the invariant.

Although it is equally possible to write down the pre-condition separately in Z and to prove this well-formedness theorem, the VDM style provides an encouragement to do it, and by requiring the final values of all state components to be specified, the VDM style helps to keep components from being forgotten. Having a separate pre-condition also makes it easier to formulate rules for proving the correctness of implementations.

The *FindPhone* operation is specified in VDM as follows:

> *FindPhone*(*name*: *NAME*) *number*: *PHONE*
> **ext rd** *known*: **set of** *NAME*
>   **rd** *phone*: **map** *NAME* **to** *PHONE*
> **pre** *name* ∈ *known*
> **post** *number* = *phone*(*name*).

Again the relevant state components are listed, but this time they are marked as read-only (**rd**); this implies that their final values are equal to the initial values, so this fact does not need to be stated explicitly in the post-condition. The input *name* and the output *number* are declared in a way which suggests a subroutine heading, which is convenient when operations are implemented as subroutines.

VDM does not have anything analogous to the schema-calculus in Z, which allows small specifications to be put together to make larger ones. It is possible to 'quote' the pre- and post-conditions of one operation in describing another, but operation specifications are not regarded as self-contained objects which can be combined to make new ones.

There are, however, many similarities between Z and VDM, both in the style of the methods and in the mathematics used to support them. Both use ordinary mathematical structures—sets, functions, and sequences—to model data, and the notation of predicate logic to describe operations on the data. In both methods, a specification typically consists of the description of a state space followed by the description of operations which change the state.

1.4.2 *Algebraic specifications*
Algebraic specifications begin with a world which is far simpler than the rich universe of structured types assumed by Z and VDM. Their basic vocabulary is just some named sets and some total functions on these sets. Specifications

describe the properties these functions are required to satisfy, typically by giving equations which relate the functions to each other.

As an example, here is the telephone number database specified once more, this time in the algebraic specification language Clear. The specification starts with the two basic types, names and telephone numbers. We need to be able to tell if two names are the same, so names come equipped with an equality test:

> **const** *Name* =
>   **enrich** *Bool* **by**
>   **sorts** *name*
>   **opns** $\_ == \_ : name, name \rightarrow bool$
>   **eqns** $n == n = true$
> $n == m = m == n$
> $n == m \land m == p \Rightarrow n == p = true$
>   **enden**

This theory, a fragment of specification in Clear, extends the theory *Bool* of booleans with a new named set or sort *name*, and a binary operation == taking a pair of names to a boolean: it is the equality test mentioned above. Three equations specify that the equality test must be an equivalence relation on names.

For telephone numbers, no equality test is needed, but there must be a special number *unknown* which is the result of trying to find a name not in the database.

> **const** *Phone* =
>   **theory**
>   **sorts** *phone*
>   **opns** *unknown* : *phone*
>   **endth**

Error elements like *unknown* are made necessary in algebraic specifications by the requirement that all operations be total: when an operation is applied outside its intended domain of applicability, an error element is the result. The specification language is sometimes provided with special facilities for introducing error elements and implicitly requiring all operations to be *strict* in the sense that any operation applied to error elements will itself return an error element. Some work has also been done with algebraic specifications of partial functions (Wirsing & Broy, 1982).

Possible states of the database are described in terms of the way they can be created. The initial state is the database *empty* containing no telephone numbers, and a new state can be made from an old one by adding a new name and number with the operation *addphone*. This operation takes three arguments, a name, a telephone number and a database, and returns the result of adding the name and number to the database.

The theory *Database* joins the theories of names and telephone numbers, and enriches them with a sort *db* of databases and operations *empty*, and *addphone*. The operation *empty* is a constant of sort *db*: it can be thought of as a function which takes no arguments.

> **const** *Database* =
>   **enrich** *Name* + *Phone* **by**
>   **data sorts** *db*
>   **opns** *empty* : *db*
>   *addphone* : *name*, *number*, *db* $\rightarrow$ *db*
>   **eqns** *addphone*$(n, x, addphone(n, y, d))$
>   = *addphone*(n, y, d)
>   *addphone*$(n, x, addphone(m, y, d))$
>   = *addphone*$(m, y, addphone(n, x, d))$
>   **if** $not(n == m)$
>   **enden**

The keyword **data** indicates that we are describing here exactly what databases there are. It means that there are no elements of *db* except those which can be generated by starting with the empty database and repeatedly adding new names and numbers. The elements generated in this way are distinct unless the equations require otherwise. The two equations say that if two numbers are added for the same name, the one added second replaces that added first, and that, provided two names are different, it does not matter in what order they are added to the database. So each database expression can be reduced to a canonical form in which each name is added at most once, and two expressions of this form are equal if they differ only in the order of adding names.

This description of the database states contrasts sharply with the description given in the Z and VDM specifications: there, an explicit model for states was given in terms of sets and functions, and here, the states are described implicitly as those objects which can be generated by applying certain operations, the operations being specified by equations.

The specification of the database system is completed by adding the operation *findphone* for looking up telephone numbers. This takes as arguments a name and a database, and returns the number associated with the name in the database if there is one, and *unknown* otherwise.

> **const** *PhoneDB* =
>   **enrich** *Database* **by**
>   **opns** *findphone* : *name*, *db* → *number*
>   **eqns** *findphone*(*n*, *addphone*(*n*, *x*, *d*)) = *x*
>   *findphone*(*n*, *addphone*(*m*, *x*, *d*))
>   = *findphone*(*n*, *d*) **if** *not*(*n* == *m*)
>   *findphone*(*n*, *empty*) = *unknown*
>   **enden**

The equations in this theory describe the effect of *findphone* by showing how it acts on databases generated in various ways with *addphone* and *empty*. The result of looking up the name n in the database *addphone*(n, x, d) is the number x, whilst the result of looking it up in *addphone*(m, x, d), where m is different from n, is the same as the result of looking it up in d. The result of looking anything up in the empty database is *unknown*.

This specification has been built up in stages from the basic theories *Name* and *Phone*. Clear provides a facility for *theory procedures*, which can have such basic theories as formal parameters. For example, the database specification might be made into a theory procedure with the following procedure heading:

> **proc** *PhoneDB*(*Name* : *Ident*, *Phone* : *Triv*) =
>   . . .

The *meta-sorts* of the parameters, *Ident* and *Triv*, give requirements on the formal parameter theories *Name* and *Phone*: both must have a sort *element*, and *Name* must in addition have an equality test ==. If the specification is cast in this form, it can then be applied to various actual parameters to specify different versions of the database. For example, a database in which the names are strings and the telephone numbers are natural numbers is specified by the expression

> *PhoneDB*(*String*[*element* **is** *string*], *Nat*[*element* **is** *nat*]).

The actual parameters are the theories *String* of strings and *Nat* of natural numbers, and the sorts *string* and *nat* have been identified as corresponding to the formal parameter's sort *element* in each case.

This construction is especially useful for specifying basic data types such as sets and sequences. If these are cast as theory procedures, then specifications may talk about sequences of characters, sequences of natural numbers, sets of sequences of natural numbers, and so on. A slight inconvenience is that many sorts may then have the same name. For example, both sequences of characters and sequences of numbers would form sorts called *sequence*, and both names and telephone numbers in the theory procedure above form sorts called *element*. References to these sorts must be disambiguated by writing e.g. *element* **of** *Name* or *element* **of** *Phone*.

These facilities make it possible to build a powerful collection of parametrized theories containing all the usual data types. The notion of a metasort allows complex requirements on parameter theories to be specified: for example, it is possible to build a theory of sorting in which the parameter describes not only the kind of objects to be sorted but also the ordering relation to be used for the sorting. Such a theory procedure can only be applied to actual parameters which satisfy the requirements: in this case, the relation supplied as part of the actual parameter must really be an ordering relation. This degree of generality in parametrization is not easy to achieve in Z; on the other hand, Z allows higher-order functions, and many concepts which Clear would describe with theory procedures can be described in Z using these. For example, sorting can be described as a higher-order function which maps ordering relations to functions from sequences to sequences.

1.5   Overview

Here is a brief summary of the contents of each chapter:

Chapter 2: Basic Concepts. Beginning with a presentation of axiomatic set theory as a Z specification, the chapter builds up the notion of type, then introduces the model-theoretic notions needed to build semantic domains for Z. The style of denotational semantics to be used for the definition of Z is first discussed from a mathematical point of view, then illustrated with an example from the language of schema-expressions.

Chapter 3: The Semantics of Z. The particular semantic domains needed for Z are defined, and semantic functions are given, linking the abstract syntax of a Z-like specification language to operations on the domains. The object language is chosen to reflect as accurately as possible the Z notation as it is currently used, but to be as simple as possible. First, a model of nested scopes is set up: this works by having each variable tagged with the lexical level of its declaration. Then the structure of the environment of a Z specification is described. Finally, the semantic functions are defined for each syntactic class.

Chapter 4: Discussion. A discussion of various issues in the design of Z. The most important of these is a construct for defining global constants with generic parameters; this construct is widely used in Z practice for building up a tool-kit of mathematical definitions. The extent to which the semantics respects referential transparency, and the way it treats partially defined terms are also discussed, and the semantic basis of Z is compared with that of Clear.

Chapter 5: Studies in Z Style. Some topics connected with the use of formal specifications. First, the problem of reasoning about complex specifications is examined, and a style of reasoning is suggested in which the structure of proofs about a specification is made to reflect the structure of the specification itself. Next, the specification of the basic types used in Z specifications is discussed, using the natural numbers as an example; this shows how a mathematical theory can be developed in Z in such a way that its consistency can be proved. Third, the relationship between specifications and programs is examined, and finally an example is given to show how abstraction from implementation details makes non-determinism necessary in specifications.

Chapters 4 and 5 contain several applications of the semantic theory developed in chapters 2 and 3, and it may be helpful to begin to read them before finishing the earlier chapters. The applications provide motivation for the development of the theory, and illustrations of the main ideas. At the back of the book are a brief description of the Z notation and glossary of the standard mathematical symbols, and an index of the names defined in the formal semantics.

CHAPTER TWO

BASIC CONCEPTS

The aim of this chapter is to introduce the concepts needed for a formal semantics of Z: that is, to map out the meta-linguistic ideas and the semantic structures which underlie the notation. Z is a set-theoretic specification language, and the chapter begins, appropriately enough, by describing a 'world' of sets in which the constructs of Z can be explained: this world of sets is a weakened version of Zermelo-Fraenkel set theory. Next, the Z system of types is introduced, and the semantics of types is given in terms of the (untyped) world of sets. The next two sections describe the basic semantic structures of Z: signatures, structures and varieties, and the notation used for the semantic description in chapter 3. The chapter finishes with a small example, in which the semantics of some basic operations on schemas is given in the denotational style.

2.1 The world of sets

Specifications in Z describe sets, and its constructs have their meaning in operations on sets. This makes it natural to start an account of the semantics of Z by describing what sets there are, what essential properties they have, and what operations can be performed on them. Mathematicians have established the foundations of set theory as an axiomatic theory of first-order logic. One of the axiom systems, ZF, is due to Zermelo and Fraenkel, and we shall adopt it as a specification for a 'world' of sets in which the operations of Z can be explained. An elementary introduction to Zermelo-Fraenkel set theory is given in the book (Enderton, 1977).

The ZF axioms describe a universe of 'pure' sets in which everything is a set: this universe can be conceived as being built up starting with just the empty set. At first sight, this seems unlikely to lead to an acceptable foundation for mathematics, for, as we know, mathematics is intimately concerned with the properties of natural numbers, real numbers, tuples, and so on, and these objects do not at first sight seem to be sets. In fact, it is possible to describe an 'impure' set theory in which the construction of sets starts with certain objects which are not themselves sets—these set-theoretic 'atoms' might include the natural numbers, for example.

Although such an approach is possible, it is not necessary, because it turns out that any mathematical structure can be mimicked by an isomorphic structure built from pure sets alone—as we shall see later, both the natural numbers and the operation of tuple-formation can be modelled in this way. There might seem to be a possibility of confusion between a set itself and the same set regarded as representing, say, a natural number, but this confusion is avoided in ordinary mathematical usage by notational conventions; in the Z notation, the system of types provides formal means for avoiding the confusion.

2.1.1 *Sets and membership*

A specification for the world of sets can be obtained by taking each of the ZF axioms and defining in Z a corresponding operation on sets. Take as an example the *union* axiom:

$$\forall x. \, \exists y. \, \forall z. \, z \in y \Leftrightarrow (\exists w. \, z \in w \wedge w \in x).$$

This says that for each set x, there is a set y whose elements are exactly the elements of elements of x. The extensional property of membership means that any two sets with the same elements are the same, and since in the union axiom, the elements of y are determined exactly in terms of x, this means that y is uniquely determined in terms of x. So the union axiom unambiguously defines an operation on sets taking x to y: it is the 'generalized union' operation $\bigcup$.

Now let W stand for the 'world' of sets, and let $\in$ stand for the membership relation on W. An important property of $\in$ is its extensionality, that any two sets with the same elements are equal:

$[W]$

$$\_\in\_ : W \leftrightarrow W$$
$$\forall x, y : W \bullet (\forall z : W \bullet z \in x \Leftrightarrow z \in y) \Rightarrow x = y.$$

The union operation can be defined as a function from W to W:

$$union : W \to W$$
$$\forall x, y : W \bullet$$
$$y \in union(x) \Leftrightarrow (\exists z : W \bullet y \in z \land z \in x).$$

The other operations of set theory can be described in a similar way: this is done in detail below.

By formulating the axioms of set theory in this way, we obtain a specification in Z which describes a world of sets W and a collection of set-theoretic operations taking sets in W to other sets in W. But there is a problem with consistency. Since W is a given-set name in a Z specification, it must denote a set, and it is well-known that paradoxes result if we suppose that the totality of all sets is itself a set: Russell's paradox is one of them. In fact, consistency of the 'world of sets' specification does not require that W contain all sets, but just that it be closed under the operations of set theory described in the specification. If the axiom of *replacement* is omitted from the specification, there are indeed sets with this closure property—they are known as 'natural models' of ZF-without-replacement, and an example is the set $V_{\omega+\omega}$ in the cumulative hierarchy (Enderton, 1977, chapter 9).

A related remark concerns the assumptions needed to prove consistency of the specification. Gödel's second incompleteness theorem means that there is no possibility of proving the consistency of the specification of W within the world of sets which it describes; in fact, the construction of natural models for ZF-without-replacement requires the use of the axiom of replacement itself, because it relies on transfinite recursion. The existence of natural models which satisfy the axiom of replacement as well depends on the existence of 'unreachable cardinals', and this is independent of the ZF axioms.

2.1.2   Basic operations

The other operations on sets can be specified in the same way as *union*. The *null set* axiom just asserts the existence of a set with no elements, which we call *null*:

$$null : W$$
$$\forall x : W \bullet \neg\, x \in null.$$

The *pair-sets* axiom allows the two-element set $\{x, y\}$ to be constructed for any sets x and y, and we call the operation taking x and y to the W representation of $\{x, y\}$ by the name *pair*:

$$pair : W \times W \to W$$
$$z \sqsubseteq pair(x, y) \Leftrightarrow z = x \lor z = y.$$

Of course, $pair(x, x)$ has the single element x. This allows singleton sets to be constructed; the operation *sing* taking x to the W representation of $\{x\}$ can be defined in terms of *pair*:

$$sing : W \to W$$
$$sing(x) = pair(x, x).$$

The combination of *union* and *pair* allows binary unions to be formed:

$$\_ \sqcup \_ : W \times W \to W$$
$$x \sqcup y = union(pair(x, y)).$$

A set x is a *subset* of another set y if every element of x is also an element of y:

$$\_ \sqsubseteq \_ : W \leftrightarrow W$$
$$y \sqsubseteq x \Leftrightarrow (\forall z : W \bullet z \sqsubseteq y \Rightarrow z \sqsubseteq x).$$

The *power set* axiom asserts the existence of the power set $\mathsf{P}\, x$ of any set x; its elements are just the subsets of x:

$$power : W \to W$$
$$y \sqsubseteq power(x) \Leftrightarrow y \sqsubseteq x.$$

The axiom of *infinity* ensures that there is at least one infinite set in W. There are several formulations, but we choose one which describes a certain set *bigset*, which must be infinite, for it contains $\emptyset$ and is closed under the operation taking x to $x \cup \{x\}$:

$$bigset : W$$
$$null \sqsubseteq bigset$$
$$\forall x : W \bullet x \sqsubseteq bigset \Rightarrow x \sqcup sing(x) \sqsubseteq bigset.$$

Without this axiom, there is no guarantee that the world of sets will contain an infinite set at all; the other axioms have models in which all sets are finite, for all the other operations preserve finiteness—the collection V_ω of all hereditarily finite sets is one example of such a model. The infinite set *bigset* allows the direct construction of a model of the natural numbers by pure sets, for 0 can be modelled by $\varnothing$ and $succ(x)$ by $x \cup \{x\}$.

The axiom of *separation* is actually an axiom scheme: if

$$\phi(a, b_1, \ldots, b_n)$$

is a formula of set theory with free variables among a, b_1, $\ldots$, b_n, and x, w_1, $\ldots$, w_n are sets, then the axiom asserts the existence of a set

$$y = \{\, z \in x \mid \phi(z, w_1, \ldots, w_n)\,\}.$$

For present purposes, it is enough to identify the formula ϕ with the subset of W it describes. Just as some formulae of set theory describe collections too large to be sets, so there are some subsets S of W too large to be 'represented' in W: there may be no x in W with

$$\forall z : W \bullet z \in x \Leftrightarrow z \in S.$$

This is the reason why the axiom of separation must give the set y as a subset of an already-known set x. It is modelled by the operation *filter*:

$$
\begin{array}{|l}
\textit{filter} : W \times \mathbf{P}\,W \to W \\
\hline
\forall\, x, z : W; \; S : \mathbf{P}\,W \bullet \\
\quad z \in \textit{filter}(x, S) \Leftrightarrow z \in x \wedge z \in S.
\end{array}
$$

An easy application of the operation *filter* is in the definition of binary intersection:

$$
\begin{array}{|l}
\_\sqcap\_ : W \times W \to W \\
\hline
x \sqcap y = \textit{filter}(x, \{\, z : W \mid z \in y \,\}).
\end{array}
$$

The axiom of *regularity* says that every non-empty set x has an element y which shares no element with x. It is needed for technical reasons to rule out the possibility of pathological sets which are elements of themselves, or elements of one of their own elements, and so on. Since y is not uniquely determined by x, the axiom does not give a uniquely defined operation, and it is stated here using an existential quantifier:

$$
\forall\, x : W \bullet x \neq \textit{null} \Rightarrow \\
\quad (\exists\, y : W \bullet y \in x \wedge x \sqcap y = \textit{null}).
$$

If, for example, there were a set $x : W$ with $x \in x$, then the singleton set $sing(x)$ would contradict the axiom of regularity, for its only element is x, and $x \sqcap sing(x)$ is non-empty—it has x as an element.

The remaining two axioms in ZF are the axioms of *replacement* and *choice*. Neither of these will be needed to explain the operations of Z, so they are omitted from the specification. The axiom of replacement, as noted above, must be omitted to avoid problems with the consistency of the specification.

The axiom of choice, although it could in principle be added, is rather less elementary than the others, for it involves the notion of a function, which is better treated later within the framework of Z. Much mathematics can be done without using the axiom of choice, and since it asserts the existence of an object without saying how to find it, we might expect the axiom to be of little use in programming. It should be noted that a choice principle can indeed be viewed constructively within the framework of intuitionistic logic: cf. (Martin-Löf, 1984), in which such a choice principle is proved as a theorem of intuitionistic type theory. This constructive choice principle is, however, weaker in content than the classical axiom of choice, because in intuitionistic logic, being given a family of non-empty sets entails being given an element of each member of the family.

2.1.3 *Derived operations*

The six operations *union*, *null*, *pair*, *power*, *bigset*, and *filter*, together with the axioms of extensionality and regularity, form the basis of our view of set theory. In addition to these primitive operations, some other operations for forming tuples and Cartesian products are needed in the semantics of Z. These operations could in principle be defined in terms of the primitive operations—one way of doing this would be to define an ordered pair constructor which encoded (x, y) as

$$\{\{x\}, \{x, y\}\}.$$

This encoding *couple* could be defined in terms of the primitive operations on the world of sets:

$$couple : W \times W \to W$$
$$couple(x, y) = pair(sing(x), pair(x, y)).$$

Tuples with more than two elements could then be constructed by iterating the ordered pair construction, and so on. But a different approach is taken here; the operations are characterized by axioms and not defined explicitly in terms of the basic operations. The consistency of the axiomatic presentation could be proved by using the basic operations to give an explicit construction like this one.

One derived operation takes a finite sequence of sets and forms a 'tuple' from it: the operation maps x_1, ..., x_n into a set representing in W the tuple $(x_1, \ldots, x_n)$.

$$
\begin{array}{|l}
\hline
tuple : \text{seq } W \to W \\
\hline
\forall x, y : \text{seq } W \bullet \\
\quad \#x = \#y \land tuple(x) = tuple(y) \Rightarrow x = y.
\end{array}
$$

The axiom says that for two tuples of the same length to be equal, they must have the same components. It does not require, for example, that

$$tuple \langle x, y \rangle \neq tuple \langle p, q, r \rangle.$$

This freedom allows *tuple* to be defined constructively by iterating the *couple* operation.

Another derived operation corresponds to the n-fold Cartesian product, taking sets X_1, ..., X_n to a set representing the Cartesian product $X_1 \times \cdots \times X_n$.

$$
\begin{array}{|l}
\hline
cproduct : \text{seq } W \to W \\
\hline
\forall u : W;\ X : \text{seq } W \bullet \\
\quad u \in cproduct(X) \Leftrightarrow \\
\qquad (\exists x : \text{seq } W \bullet u = tuple(x) \land \\
\qquad\quad \#x = \#X \land (\forall i : \text{dom } x \bullet x(i) \in X(i))).
\end{array}
$$

Analogous to these two operations are another two which, instead of forming tuples from sequences, operate on finite collections of named sets, that is, on finite mappings from a set *IDENT* into W. There is an operation analogous to *tuple*, which makes a 'binding' out of a collection of named objects:

$$
\begin{array}{|l}
\hline
binding : (IDENT \nrightarrow W) \to W \\
\hline
\forall x, y : IDENT \nrightarrow W \bullet \\
\quad \text{dom } x = \text{dom } y \land binding(x) = binding(y) \Rightarrow x = y.
\end{array}
$$

There is also a corresponding 'schema product' operation:

$$sproduct : (IDENT \nrightarrow W) \to W$$

$$\forall u : W; X : IDENT \nrightarrow W \bullet$$
$$\quad u \sqsubseteq sproduct(X) \Leftrightarrow$$
$$\qquad (\exists x : IDENT \nrightarrow W \bullet u = binding(x) \land$$
$$\qquad\quad \mathrm{dom}\, x = \mathrm{dom}\, X \land (\forall n : \mathrm{dom}\, x \bullet x(n) \sqsubseteq X(n))).$$

These operations will be used to explain the Z term θA, which forms a 'binding' from the components of the schema A, and the term $t.x$, which selects a component from such a binding. The *binding* operation might be defined constructively by assuming an encoding of elements of $IDENT$ as sets in W, then representing finite mappings from $IDENT$ to W by sets of ordered pairs in W.

As mentioned above, not all subsets of W are 'represented' by elements of W. The converse is true, however: each element of W represents a subset of W, and because of extensionality, this representation is unique. The 'abstraction function' is

$$abs : W \rightarrowtail \mathbf{P}\, W$$

$$abs(u) = \{\, v : W \mid v \sqsubseteq u \,\}.$$

The inverse, *rep*, defined by

$$rep : \mathbf{P}\, W \nrightarrow W$$

$$rep = abs^{-1}.$$

is of course partial, but its domain contains all the finite subsets of W:

$$\vdash \mathbf{F}\, W \subseteq \mathrm{dom}\, rep.$$

This can be proved by induction on the size of the finite set: the empty set is represented by *null*, and if S is represented by u, then $S \cup \{x\}$ is represented by $u \sqcup sing(x)$.

2.2   Types

Every variable introduced in a Z specification is given a type. There are several reasons for this. The first reason is technical, and is connected with the operation of *comprehension* by which a set can be made from any schema: if A is a schema, then $\{\, A \,\}$ is the set of all bindings made from models of A. For this to exist as a set, there must be an already-known set S in which it is included. The axiom of separation—that is, the operation *filter* in the world of sets—then allows $\{A\}$ to be obtained as a subset of S. If a type is given to each variable of A, the existence of the set S is guaranteed.

In simple cases, the existence of a suitable set S can be shown without the aid of types, provided only that the convention is followed of introducing each variable by giving a set-valued term over which it ranges. These terms can then be used to construct S. This works well for simple cases, but if a schema is obtained by applying schema operations to other schemas, it becomes difficult to identify the ranges of the variables unambiguously—this is particularly true in the case of schema negation—and under these circumstances types are needed.

Another technical reason for having types is that we wish to be free to use encodings of tuples, and so on, as objects in the world of sets, and want the properties of the encoded objects to be independent of the encoding. This can be ensured by considering only properties which can be expressed by well-typed predicates, because these will not allow the comparison of terms from different types. For example, the equation

$$(x, y) = \{\{x\}, \{x, y\}\}$$

will not be well-typed because, even if x and y have the same type X, the left-hand side of the equation will have type $X \times X$, and the right-hand side will have type $\mathsf{P}(\mathsf{P}\, X)$, and these are different. Of course, if tuples are modelled using this encoding, both sides of the equation will have the same value in the world of sets, but this is of no interest if their types are different.

Other reasons for giving types to variables have to do with the practice of reading and writing specifications. The theory of types can be made decidable, so that it is possible to check automatically that a specification is well-typed: in fact, chapter 3 contains an explicit set of rules for deriving the type of a term. Experience with programming languages shows that type-checking is a valuable way of catching minor errors, such as functions applied to the wrong number of arguments, and these errors are likely to be just as common in specifications as in programs.

2.2.1   *Syntax of types*
The simplest types are *given-set names*: these are names for sets which are assumed given, either because they are formal generic parameters of a specification, or because they are sets of basic objects whose internal structure is of no interest in the specification. It would be possible to include also some primitive types, such as the natural-numbers symbol N, but this turns

out not to be necessary, because these primitive types can themselves be specified in Z: see chapter 5. In examples, however, $\mathbb{N}$ will be used as a type.

More complex types can be built up with type-constructors: for example, if a is a type then the formal expression $\mathbb{P}\,a$ is also a type. The formal Cartesian product

$$a_1 \times \cdots \times a_n$$

of n types $a_1, \ldots, a_n$ is again a type, and there is also a special 'schema product' type

$$(\!| x_1 : a_1; \ldots; x_n : a_n |\!)$$

formed from a finite collection of named types.

In the Z notation, the abstract syntax of types can be taken as

$$
\begin{aligned}
TYPE ::= &\ givenT \langle\!\langle NAME \rangle\!\rangle \\
| &\ powerT \ \langle\!\langle TYPE \rangle\!\rangle \\
| &\ tupleT \ \langle\!\langle \mathrm{seq}\ TYPE \rangle\!\rangle \\
| &\ schemaT \langle\!\langle IDENT \twoheadrightarrow TYPE \rangle\!\rangle.
\end{aligned}
$$

This corresponds with the more informal notation as follows:

$$
\begin{aligned}
X &\ \widehat{=} \ givenT\, X \\
\mathbb{P}\,a &\ \widehat{=} \ powerT\, a \\
a_1 \times \cdots \times a_n &\ \widehat{=} \ tupleT\, \langle a_1, \ldots, a_n \rangle \\
(\!| x_1 : a_1; \ldots; x_n : a_n |\!) &\ \widehat{=} \ schemaT\, \{ x_1 \mapsto a_1, \ldots, x_n \mapsto a_n \}.
\end{aligned}
$$

The informal notation will still be used in giving examples.

Note that $X \times Y \times Z$, $X \times (Y \times Z)$, and $(X \times Y) \times Z$ are different types— no connection is assumed between n-ary Cartesian products and iterated binary products. Also, note that $(\!| x : X; y : Y |\!)$ and $(\!| y : Y; x : X |\!)$ are the same type: order of components does not matter. Finally, the abbreviation

$$(\!| x, y : X |\!) \ \widehat{=} \ (\!| x : X; y : X |\!)$$

is sometimes used.

It may be surprising at first that there is no type-constructor corresponding to the function space $X \to Y$, because we often think of variables in Z as having function types. The reason for this is that functions are identified with their graphs, so functions from X to Y are already accommodated in the type $\mathbb{P}(X \times Y)$. This is important for some applications: for example, we may know that a certain function is injective, and so wish to apply its inverse as a function, even though the inverse of a function is not in general also a function. Since it is in general undecidable whether a function described by axioms is injective, we cannot expect a type-checker to check this. On the other hand, it is possible to check the number and types of the arguments to a function, even with the weaker type system adopted here, because the type of a function from $X \times Y$ to Z, for example, will be $\mathbf{P}((X \times Y) \times Z)$, and the types of the arguments are preserved in this.

If *given* is an alphabet of names for given types, we let *Type*(*given*) be the set of all types built from names in *given*:

$$Type : \mathbf{P}\ NAME \rightarrow \mathbf{P}\ TYPE$$
$$names : TYPE \rightarrow \mathbf{P}\ NAME$$

$$Type(given) = \{\ a : TYPE \mid names(a) \subseteq given\ \}$$
$$names(givenT\ X) = \{X\}$$
$$names(powerT\ a) = names(a)$$
$$names(tupleT\ as) = \bigcup names(\!(\mathrm{ran}\ as)\!)$$
$$names(schemaT\ am) = \bigcup names(\!(\mathrm{ran}\ am)\!).$$

2.2.2 *Semantics of types*

So far, types have been regarded just as formal expressions. But the important thing about a type is that it determines a set of values which are its elements: we call this set the *carrier* of the type. If $gset : NAME \nrightarrow W$ assigns a set to each name in *given*, the carrier of each type in *Type*(*given*) can be found by interpreting the type-constructors as operations in the world of sets. We write *Carrier gset a* for the set of elements of the type a, and define this by structural recursion over the syntax of types:

$$Carrier : (NAME \nrightarrow W) \rightarrow (TYPE \nrightarrow W)$$

$$Carrier\ gset\ (givenT\ X) \cong gset(X)$$
$$Carrier\ gset\ (powerT\ a) \cong power(Carrier\ gset\ a)$$
$$Carrier\ gset\ (tupleT\ as) \cong cproduct(map\ (Carrier\ gset)\ as)$$
$$Carrier\ gset\ (schemaT\ am) \cong sproduct(map\ (Carrier\ gset)\ am).$$

(For a full explanation of the strong equality sign $\cong$, see subsection 2.4.2. Suffice it to say for now that these four equations can be read as a definition of *Carrier* by structural recursion).

It is easy to show by structural induction on types that

$$\vdash\ \mathrm{dom}\ gset = given \Rightarrow \mathrm{dom}(Carrier\ gset) = Type(given),$$

so the *Carrier* function really does define a carrier for each type over *given*.

An important characteristic of the type constructors is that they are monotonic with respect to inclusion—for example, if $A_1 \subseteq B_1$ and $A_2 \subseteq B_2$, then

$$A_1 \times A_2 \subseteq B_1 \times B_2.$$

This is important because it allows type-constructors to be applied to general terms and not just other types: for example, if t_1 is a term of type $\mathbf{P}\, B_1$ and t_2 is a term of type $\mathbf{P}\, B_2$, then $t_1 \times t_2$ is a term of type $\mathbf{P}(B_1 \times B_2)$, and the monotonicity of the Cartesian product operation $\times$ ensures that its value is an element of its type. This monotonicity property can be formalized in the following theorem:

$$\vdash\ (\forall\, G : given \bullet gset_1(G) \sqsubseteq gset_2(G)) \Rightarrow$$
$$Carrier\ gset_1\, a \sqsubseteq Carrier\ gset_2\, a.$$

2.2.3 Type substitutions

When a generic schema is instantiated with actual parameters, types are filled in for the given-set names which are its formal parameters: this means that a substitution has to take place on the types of the variables of the schema. This process is described by the function *tsubst*:

$$tsubst : (NAME \nrightarrow TYPE) \rightarrow (TYPE \nrightarrow TYPE)$$

$$tsubst\, f\, (given T\, X) \cong f(X)$$
$$tsubst\, f\, (power T\, a) \cong power T\, (tsubst\, f\, a)$$
$$tsubst\, f\, (tuple T\, as) \cong tuple T\, (map\, (tsubst\, f)\, as)$$
$$tsubst\, f\, (schema T\, am) \cong schema T\, (map\, (tsubst\, f)\, am).$$

This function has several noteworthy properties. It has the syntactic property that if the domain and range of f use certain alphabets, then so does $tsubst\, f$:

$$\vdash\ f \in given \rightarrow Type(given') \Rightarrow$$
$$tsubst\, f \in Type(given) \rightarrow Type(given').$$

This is proved by a simple structural induction, as is the following property:

$$\vdash\ f \in given \rightarrow Type(given') \wedge g \in given' \rightarrow Type(given'') \Rightarrow$$
$$(tsubst\, g) \circ (tsubst\, f) = tsubst\, ((tsubst\, g) \circ f).$$

An analogous semantic property of substitution is the following:

$$\vdash\ f \in given \rightarrow Type(given') \wedge dom\ gset = given' \Rightarrow$$
$$(Carrier\ gset) \circ (tsubst\, f) = Carrier\, ((Carrier\ gset) \circ f).$$

The proof is again by structural induction on types. We prove that

$$Carrier\ gset\ (tsubst\ f\ a) = Carrier\ ((Carrier\ gset) \circ f)\ a$$

for each type $a : Type(given)$. The base case is $a = givenT\ X$ for $X \in given$:

$$Carrier\ gset\ (tsubst\ f\ (givenT\ X))$$
$$= Carrier\ gset\ (f\ X)$$
$$= ((Carrier\ gset) \circ f)\ X$$
$$= Carrier\ ((Carrier\ gset) \circ f)\ (givenT\ X).$$

There are three step cases, for *powerT*, *tupleT* and *schemaT*. In the case $a = powerT\ a'$, where $a' : Type(given)$, we assume the result for $a = a'$, and reason as follows:

$$Carrier\ gset\ (tsubst\ f\ (powerT\ a'))$$
$$= Carrier\ gset\ (powerT\ (tsubst\ f\ a'))$$
$$= power(Carrier\ gset\ (tsubst\ f\ a'))$$
$$= power(Carrier\ ((Carrier\ gset) \circ f)\ a')\quad \text{by hypothesis}$$
$$= Carrier\ ((Carrier\ gset) \circ f)\ (powerT\ a').$$

For the case $a = tupleT\ as$ with $as : seq\ Type(given)$, we assume the result for each $a : ran\ as$, and the argument is as follows:

$$Carrier\ gset\ (tsubst\ f\ (tupleT\ as))$$
$$= Carrier\ gset\ (tupleT\ (map\ (tsubst\ f)\ as))$$
$$= cproduct\ (map\ (Carrier\ gset)\ (map\ (tsubst\ f)\ as))$$
$$= cproduct\ (map\ ((Carrier\ gset) \circ (tsubst\ f))\ as)$$
$$= cproduct\ (map\ (Carrier\ ((Carrier\ gset) \circ f))\ as)\quad \text{by hypothesis}$$
$$= Carrier\ ((Carrier\ gset) \circ f)\ (tupleT\ as).$$

The *schemaT* case is similar.

2.3   Signatures, structures, and varieties

The declarative information in a schema is captured in its *signature*: this records the names of the schema's components or local variables, their types, and the given-set names assumed by the schema. Signatures are finite objects, and are thus suitable for mechanical representation and manipulation; a simple type-checker for Z might calculate the signatures of schemas, and check the types of terms against the signature using the well-typing rules in chapter 3.

But a schema contains more information than just the declarations; the axiom part of the schema can describe a relationship among the variables, and this information can be captured by describing which *structures*—assignments of values to the variables—satisfy the axiom part.

A signature together with a class of appropriately shaped structures is called a *variety*, and varieties are used as a semantic domain for schemas in the semantics of chapter 3.

2.3.1 *Signatures*

A signature defines an alphabet of given-set names, from which types can be built, and an alphabet of variables names, and it assigns a type to each variable:

```
_SIG _____
 given : F NAME
 vars : F NAME
 type : NAME ↦ TYPE
 _____
 type ∈ vars → Type(given)
```

The axiom says that the typing function *type* assigns a type to exactly those variables in the alphabet *vars*, and that these types are formed from the given-set names in the alphabet *given*. The signature of a schema may be regarded as an interface allowing it to be put together with other schemas to form a larger specification. It also contains the information needed for type-checking a specification. The following is a simple example of a schema:

```
_A[X, Y] _____
 p : X
 q : X × Y
 _____
 ∃ y : Y • q = (p, y)
```

This has given-set names X and Y, and variables p and q. The signature of the schema A is

$\mu SIG \mid$
$\quad given = \{`X', `Y'\} \land$
$\quad vars = \{`p', `q'\} \land$
$\quad type = \{`p' \mapsto `X', `q' \mapsto tupleT \, (`X', `Y')\}.$

In this simple example, all the information above the horizontal line is captured in the signature, but in more complicated examples, this may not be the case. If, for example, $f : X \to Y$ is a variable declared to be a function, then the type of f will be $\mathbf{P}(X \times Y)$, and the fact that f is a function rather than just a relation from X to Y will be reflected in the class of structures for the schema, rather than in the type.

We say that a signature Σ_1 is a *sub-signature* of Σ_2 if the given-set names and variables of Σ_1 are also in Σ_2, and the variables have the same types:

$$
\begin{array}{|l}
\_\,subsig\,\_ : SIG \leftrightarrow SIG \\
\hline
\Sigma_1 \; subsig \; \Sigma_2 \Leftrightarrow \\
\quad \Sigma_1.given \subseteq \Sigma_2.given \wedge \\
\quad \Sigma_1.vars \subseteq \Sigma_2.vars \wedge \\
\quad \Sigma_1.type \subseteq \Sigma_2.type.
\end{array}
$$

Of course, the relation subsig is a partial ordering on signatures. The least signature under this ordering is the null signature *null_sig* with no given-set names and no variables, and two signatures in which the common variables have the same types have a least upper bound obtained by taking the union of the alphabets and of the typing functions:

$$
\begin{array}{|l}
join : SIG \times SIG \nrightarrow SIG \\
\hline
join = \\
\quad \lambda\,\Sigma_1, \Sigma_2 : SIG \mid \\
\quad\quad (\forall\, v : \Sigma_1.vars \cap \Sigma_2.vars \bullet \Sigma_1.type(v) = \Sigma_2.type(v)) \bullet \\
\quad \mu\,SIG \mid \\
\quad\quad given = \Sigma_1.given \cup \Sigma_2.given \wedge \\
\quad\quad vars = \Sigma_1.vars \cup \Sigma_2.vars \wedge \\
\quad\quad type = \Sigma_1.type \cup \Sigma_2.type.
\end{array}
$$

2.3.2 *Structures and varieties*
The information below the horizontal dividing line—the axiom part of a schema—is captured by regarding sentences as determining a class of 'structures'. Taking the schema A as an example again, the structure

‘X’ $\mapsto$ $\mathbf{N}$
‘Y’ $\mapsto$ $\{a, b, c\}$
‘p’ $\mapsto$ 3
‘q’ $\mapsto$ $(3, b)$

satisfies the axiom, but the structure

$$'X' \mapsto \{f, g, h\}$$
$$'Y' \mapsto \{a, b, c\}$$
$$'p' \mapsto h$$
$$'q' \mapsto (g, b),$$

although it also accords with the signature, fails to satisfy the axiom, because the value of p is not the same as the first component of the value of q.

So a structure takes certain given-set names and variables and gives them values in the world of sets:

```
_STRUCT_____
  gset : NAME ↦ W
  val : NAME ↦ W
_____
```

The mapping *gset* is used to interpret given-set names, and *val* is used to interpret variables.

The first requirement on the structures for a schema is that they be consistent with the signature: the domains of the *gset* and *val* mappings should be the alphabets of the signature, and the value given to each variable must be an element of its type. We define the function *Struct* to give the set of structures consistent with a signature:

```
| Struct : SIG → P STRUCT
|_____
|  Struct =
|    λ SIG • { STRUCT |
|        dom gset = given ∧
|        dom val = vars ∧
|        (∀ v : vars • val v ∈ Carrier gset (type v)) }.
```

Now a variety—the meaning of a schema—can be defined as a signature together with a set of structures for the signature:

```
_VARIETY_____
  sig : SIG
  models : P STRUCT
_____
  models ⊆ Struct(sig)
_____
```

The set *models* will typically be smaller than *Struct(sig)* because some structures will fail to satisfy the axioms of the schema. For example, the models component of the variety characterized by the schema A contains only those structures for its signature which satisfy the property

$$\exists \, yy : W \mid yy \sqsubseteq gset(`Y`) \bullet$$
$$val(`q`) = tuple \, \langle val(`p`), yy \rangle$$

expressed by the axiom of A.

If Σ_1 is a sub-signature of Σ_2, then for each structure M for Σ_2, a structure

$$restrict \, \Sigma_1 \, M$$

for Σ_1 can be found by restricting the *gset* and *val* mappings appropriately:

> $restrict : SIG \rightarrow STRUCT \nrightarrow STRUCT$
> ___
> $restrict \, \Sigma \, M \cong$
> $\mu \, M' : Struct(\Sigma) \mid$
> $M'.gset = \Sigma.given \lhd M.gset \land$
> $M'.val = \Sigma.vars \lhd M.gset.$

The following properties hold:

$$\vdash \, \Sigma_1 \text{ subsig } \Sigma_2 \Rightarrow Struct(\Sigma_2) \subseteq dom(restrict \, \Sigma_1),$$
$$\vdash \, \Sigma_1 \text{ subsig } \Sigma_2 \land \Sigma_2 \text{ subsig } \Sigma_3 \land M \in Struct(\Sigma_3) \Rightarrow$$
$$restrict \, \Sigma_1 \, (restrict \, \Sigma_2 \, M) = restrict \, \Sigma_1 \, M.$$

So restriction to a sub-signature is always possible, and restricting in two small steps is the same as restricting in one large one.

We say a variety V_1 is a *sub-variety* of V_2 if $V_1.sig$ is a sub-signature of $V_2.sig$, and the structures obtained by restricting models of V_2 are all models of V_1:

> $\_ subvar \_ : VARIETY \leftrightarrow VARIETY$
> ___
> $V_1 \text{ subvar } V_2 \Leftrightarrow$
> $V_1.sig \text{ subsig } V_2.sig \land$
> $restrict \, V_1.sig \, (\!| V_2.models |\!) \subseteq V_1.models.$

If this is the case, then V_2 has all the names of V_1, and each property shared by all the models of V_1 continues to hold in V_2. In particular, if V_2 is obtained from V_1 by adding new variables and constraining their values and those of the existing variables, then V_1 will be a sub-variety of V_2.

A simple operation on varieties is to rename their given-set names and variables; we assume that the renaming functions are injective to avoid problems with clashing names. The given-set names and variables are renamed, and the types of new variables are obtained by substituting the new given-set names into the types of the corresponding old variables. There is one model in the new variety for each model in the old—it is obtained by composing the *gset* and *val* mappings with the renaming functions.

$$
\begin{aligned}
&rename : (NAME \rightarrowtail NAME) \times (NAME \rightarrowtail NAME) \\
&\hspace{3cm} \rightarrow (VARIETY \rightarrowtail VARIETY)
\end{aligned}
$$

$$
\begin{aligned}
&rename(gm, vm) = \\
&\quad \lambda\, VARIETY \mid \\
&\qquad given \subseteq \mathrm{dom}\, gm \,\wedge\, vars \subseteq \mathrm{dom}\, vm \,\bullet \\
&\quad \mu\, VARIETY' \mid \\
&\qquad sig'.given = gm\!\left(\!sig.given\!\right) \wedge \\
&\qquad sig'.vars = vm\!\left(\!sig.vars\!\right) \wedge \\
&\qquad sig'.type \circ vm = (tsubst\,(givenT \circ gm)) \circ sig.type \wedge \\
&\qquad models' = \\
&\qquad\quad \{\, M' : Struct(sig') \mid \\
&\qquad\qquad (\exists\, M : models \,\bullet \\
&\qquad\qquad\quad M.gset = M'.gset \circ gm \wedge \\
&\qquad\qquad\quad M.val = M'.val \circ vm)\, \}.
\end{aligned}
$$

We can check that the values of variables in the new models do in fact lie in the carriers of their types. Let M and M' be as in the definition, so that

$$M.gset = M'.gset \circ gm$$

$$M.val = M'.val \circ vm.$$

For any $X : sig'.given$,

$$M'.gset\, X = Carrier\, M'.gset\,(givenT\, X),$$

so

$$M'.gset = (Carrier\, M'.gset) \circ givenT.$$

Now if $v' \in sig'.vars$, say $v' = vm\, v$ with $v \in sig.vars$, then

$$
\begin{aligned}
M'.val\, v' \\
&= M'.val\,(vm\, v) \\
&= M.val\, v \\
&\in Carrier\, M.gset\,(sig.type\, v) \\
&= Carrier\,(M'.gset \circ gm)\,(sig.type\, v) \\
&= Carrier\,((Carrier\, M'.gset) \circ givenT \circ gm)\,(sig.type\, v)
\end{aligned}
$$

$$= Carrier\ M'.gset\ (tsubst\ (given\,T \circ gm)\ (sig.type\ v)),$$

by the property of *tsubst* proved in subsection 2.2.3.

$$= Carrier\ M'.gset\ (sig'.type\ (vm\ v))$$

$$= Carrier\ M'.gset\ (sig'.type\ v'),$$

so $M'.val\ v \sqsubseteq Carrier\ M'.gset\ (sig'.type\ v)$ as required.

2.4   Notation for denotational semantics

The notation used in chapter 3 for writing semantic descriptions is closely
based on Z, but with a few special-purpose extensions. The semantics is
based on sets rather than Scott domains, and merits the name 'denotational'
because it follows the style in which the meaning of a composite phrase is
defined in terms of the meaning of its immediate constituents.

2.4.1   *Abstract syntax notation*

As our first extension, we adapt the abstract syntax notation of Z to allow constructors which mimic the intended concrete syntax of the object
language. So instead of giving the syntax of expressions as, say,

$$
\begin{aligned}
EXP ::=\ &var\ \langle\!\langle IDENT \rangle\!\rangle \\
         |\ &plus\ \langle\!\langle EXP \times EXP \rangle\!\rangle \\
         |\ &times\ \langle\!\langle EXP \times EXP \rangle\!\rangle
\end{aligned}
$$

we might write the following:

$$
\begin{aligned}
EXP ::=\ &IDENT \\
         |\ &EXP + EXP \\
         |\ &EXP * EXP.
\end{aligned}
$$

If these production rules were regarded as a context-free grammar, the resulting language would be ambiguous—in the above example, the string
'$x + y * z$' could be parsed as either '$(x + y) * z$' or '$x + (y * z)$'—but we
don't regard this ambiguity as important, because the intention is still that
the production rules describe certain tree structures.

When constructors from the abstract syntax are applied, the resulting
term is written in open-face square brackets $[\!|\ \ |\!]$, as is usual in denotational
semantics. So the notation

$$[\!| (e_1 + e_2) * e_3 |\!]$$

means the same as

$$times(plus(e_1, e_2), e_3)$$

in the conventional notation. This extension to Z helps to make the semantic equations more readable; the definitions could in principle all be written using the conventional notation, but the result would be a loss of clarity and no real gain in rigour.

2.4.2 *Strong equality*

The second extension is the use of the strong equality sign $\cong$ in defining partial functions. The normal convention in Z is that an equation

$$t_1 = t_2$$

'makes sense' only when both t_1 and t_2 are defined. This means that the specification

$$\begin{array}{|l}
f, g, h : \mathsf{N} \nrightarrow \mathsf{N} \\
\hline
\forall x : \mathsf{N} \bullet f(x) = g(x) + h(x)
\end{array}$$

says very little about the relationship between f, g and h: it says only that the value of f is the sum of the values of g and h when all three are defined. If, at some value of x, the three functions are not all defined, the equation just doesn't make sense. In a typical specification, an extra axiom would be added to fix the domains of the functions.

$$\begin{array}{|l}
f, g, h : \mathsf{N} \rightarrow \mathsf{N} \\
\hline
\operatorname{dom} f = \operatorname{dom} g \cap \operatorname{dom} h \\
\forall x : \operatorname{dom} f \bullet f(x) = g(x) + h(x).
\end{array}$$

This need for an extra axiom may be no bad thing in ordinary specifications, for the domain of a partial function is an important piece of information, and is often worth recording explicitly. But in denotational semantics, one often needs to define a function whose domain is identical with the domain of definition of an expression, and it becomes tedious to write out an explicit axiom to fix the domain. In such situations, the strong equality sign $\cong$ can be used; the equation

$$t_1 \cong t_2$$

is true when *either* both t_1 and t_2 are defined and they have the same value, *or* both are undefined, and is false otherwise. This means that the specification

$$\begin{array}{|l} f, g, h : \mathbb{N} \nrightarrow \mathbb{N} \\ \hline \forall x : \mathbb{N} \bullet f(x) \cong g(x) + h(x). \end{array}$$

is wholly equivalent to the second of those above: in particular, $f(x)$ will be defined just when $g(x) + h(x)$ is defined, i.e. just when both $g(x)$ and $h(x)$ are defined. In consequence, $\operatorname{dom} f = \operatorname{dom} g \cap \operatorname{dom} h$. More will be said about the semantics of equality between partially defined terms in chapter 4.

In conjunction with the strong equality sign, it is useful to have a strict functional *map* for mapping a sequence through a partial function. This is defined as follows; I is the index type (natural numbers in the case of ordinary sequences), and X and Y are the types of the argument and result respectively.

$$\begin{array}{|l} \underline{[I, X, Y]} \\ \quad map : (X \nrightarrow Y) \rightarrow (I \nrightarrow X) \nrightarrow (I \nrightarrow Y) \\ \hline \quad map\, f = (\lambda s : I \nrightarrow X \mid \operatorname{ran} s \subseteq \operatorname{dom} f \bullet f \circ s) \end{array}$$

The important difference between $f \circ s$ and $map\, f\, s$ is best shown by an example. If *pred* is the inverse of the successor function on $\mathbb{N}$—so its domain is $\mathbb{N} \setminus \{0\}$—we have

$$\begin{aligned} pred &\circ \langle 2, 4, 3, 0 \rangle \\ &= pred \circ \{1 \mapsto 2, 2 \mapsto 4, 3 \mapsto 3, 4 \mapsto 0\} \\ &= \{1 \mapsto 1, 2 \mapsto 3, 3 \mapsto 2\} \\ &= \langle 1, 3, 2 \rangle, \end{aligned}$$

so *pred* $\circ \langle 2, 4, 3, 0 \rangle$ is defined, and is even a well-formed sequence, even though 0, an element of the original sequence, is not in the domain of *pred*. On the other hand, the extra condition on arguments of *map pred* means that *map pred* $\langle 2, 4, 3, 0 \rangle$ is undefined, because 0 is in the range of the sequence but not in the domain of *pred*.

2.4.3 *Example: arithmetic expressions*

These two ideas—abstract syntax notation and strong equality—can be put together to give a semantics for arithmetic expressions. We adopt the abstract syntax defined above, and let an environment be a partial function from identifiers to $\mathbb{N}$:

$$ENV \,\, \hat{=} \,\, IDENT \rightarrowtail \mathbb{N}$$

Now the meaning of expressions is given by the semantic function *exp*:

$$exp : ENV \rightarrow EXP \rightarrowtail \mathbb{N}$$

$$exp \, \rho \, [x] \cong \rho(x)$$
$$exp \, \rho \, [e_1 + e_2] \cong exp \, \rho \, [e_1] + exp \, \rho \, [e_2]$$
$$exp \, \rho \, [e_1 * e_2] \cong exp \, \rho \, [e_1] * exp \, \rho \, [e_2].$$

The use of strong equality in the semantic equations ensures that $exp \, \rho \, [e]$ is defined exactly when all the identifiers in e are in the domain of ρ.

This definition deviates from the usual 'Oxford' style in making the expression to be evaluated the last argument of the curried function *exp* rather than the first. The reason for this stems from an extensional property of domains which is not shared by sets. In domain theory (with a suitable definition of the function space) the two functions $f, g : D \rightarrow (E \rightarrow F)$ defined by

$$f = \lambda \, d : D. \, \bot_{E \rightarrow F}$$
$$g = \lambda \, d : D. \, \lambda \, e : E. \, \bot_F$$

are equal by extensionality, for $f \, d \, e = \bot_F = g \, d \, e$. But in set theory, the analogous pair of functions $f, g : S \rightarrowtail T \rightarrowtail U$ defined by

$$f = \varnothing$$
$$g = \{\, s : S \bullet (s, \varnothing) \,\}$$

are certainly different: they have different graphs. This means that an equation

$$h \, s \, t \cong \langle \text{an expression in } s \text{ and } t \rangle$$

might not define h exactly—for example, if the expression is always undefined, then h might be either of the two functions f and g defined above. In view of this, it is convenient to make all the arrows in the type of a semantic function total except for the last; this convention makes the last parameter rather special, so we choose it to be the syntactic parameter, which is rather special anyway.

2.4.4 *Partial recursion*

Although the semantic equations for expressions presented above read just
as one would expect, the questions arise whether such recursive definitions
of partial functions always have a solution, and if so, whether the solution is
unique. Let us take a recursive definition of a partial function on the natural
numbers and extract its mathematical content. Assuming, for some set X,
a constant $a : X$ and a partial function $G : \mathbb{N} \times X \twoheadrightarrow X$, we might attempt
to define a partial function $f : \mathbb{N} \twoheadrightarrow X$ by the equations

$$f(0) \cong a$$
$$\forall n : \mathbb{N} \bullet f(n+1) \cong G(n, f(n)).$$

The first of these equations says that $0 \in \operatorname{dom} f$ and $f(0) = a$, and the
second says firstly that $f(n+1)$ is defined, i.e. $n+1 \in \operatorname{dom} f$, exactly when
$G(n, f(n))$ is defined, i.e. $n \in \operatorname{dom} f$ and $(n, f(n)) \in \operatorname{dom} G$, and secondly
that in this case,

$$f(n+1) = G(n, f(n)).$$

So the existence and uniqueness of a partial function f satisfying the recursive definition follows from the following theorem, a slight generalization of
the usual recursion theorem dealing with total functions.

Theorem (Partial recursion on $\mathbb{N}$). *Let X be a set, and suppose $a : X$
and $G : \mathbb{N} \times X \twoheadrightarrow X$. Then there is a unique partial function $f : \mathbb{N} \twoheadrightarrow X$
such that*

(i) $0 \in \operatorname{dom} f$,

(ii) $f(0) = a$,

(iii) $\forall n : \mathbb{N} \bullet n+1 \in \operatorname{dom} f \Leftrightarrow n \in \operatorname{dom} f \wedge (n, f(n)) \in \operatorname{dom} G$, *and*

(iv) $\forall n : \mathbb{N} \bullet n+1 \in \operatorname{dom} f \Rightarrow f(n+1) = G(n, f(n))$.

Proof: We say that $h : \mathbb{N} \twoheadrightarrow X$ is an *attempt* if

(a) $0 \in \operatorname{dom} h \Rightarrow h(0) = a$, and

(b) $\forall n : \mathbb{N} \bullet n+1 \in \operatorname{dom} h \Rightarrow$
$\qquad n \in \operatorname{dom} h \wedge (n, h(n)) \in \operatorname{dom} G \wedge h(n+1) = G(n, h(n))$.

The idea is that an attempt is a function which satisfies conditions (i)–(iv)
except that its domain may be too small.

We first show that *any two attempts agree on their common domain.* Let h and h' be attempts. We show by induction that for any $n : \mathsf{N}$,

$$n \in \operatorname{dom} h \cap \operatorname{dom} h' \Rightarrow h(n) = h'(n). \tag{$*$}$$

If $0 \in \operatorname{dom} h \cap \operatorname{dom} h'$ then $h(0) = a = h'(0)$ by (a). Now assume $(*)$ holds for some value of n, and suppose that $n + 1 \in \operatorname{dom} h \cap \operatorname{dom} h'$. Then $n \in \operatorname{dom} h \cap \operatorname{dom} h'$ by (b), so by $(*)$, $h(n) = h'(n)$. It follows that

$$h(n + 1) = G(n, h(n)) = G(n, h'(n)) = h'(n + 1).$$

Let $f : \mathsf{N} \twoheadrightarrow X$ be defined by

$$f = \bigcup \{ h : \mathsf{N} \twoheadrightarrow X \mid h \text{ is an attempt} \}.$$

We claim that f *is itself an attempt.* For if $0 \in \operatorname{dom} f$, then $0 \in \operatorname{dom} h$ for some attempt h, and $f(0) = h(0) = a$. Also, if $n + 1 \in \operatorname{dom} f$, then $n + 1 \in \operatorname{dom} h$ for some attempt h, and so $n \in \operatorname{dom} h \subseteq \operatorname{dom} f$, and $(n, f(n)) = (n, h(n)) \in \operatorname{dom} G$. So

$$f(n + 1) = h(n + 1) = G(n, h(n)) = G(n, f(n)).$$

Moreover, f *satisfies* (i)–(iv). For $\{0 \mapsto a\}$ is an attempt, so $0 \in \operatorname{dom} f$, and f satisfies (i), and hence (ii) by (a). Suppose $n \in \operatorname{dom} f$ and $(n, f(n)) \in \operatorname{dom} G$, but $n + 1 \notin \operatorname{dom} f$. Let

$$h = f \cup \{n + 1 \mapsto G(n, f(n))\}.$$

Plainly h is also an attempt, and $n + 1 \in \operatorname{dom} h$, so $n + 1 \in \operatorname{dom} f$, which is a contradiction. So f satisfies (iii) and also (iv) by (b).

Lastly, *the solution f to $(*)$ is unique.* For suppose f and f' both satisfy $(*)$. Then *a fortiori* both are attempts, and so they agree on their common domain. It remains to show that f and f' have the same domain, and we do this by proving inductively that for all $n : \mathsf{N}$,

$$n \in \operatorname{dom} f \Leftrightarrow n \in \operatorname{dom} f'.$$

Since $0 \in \operatorname{dom} f \cap \operatorname{dom} f'$, this holds for $n = 0$. Assume for some value of n that $n \in \operatorname{dom} f \Leftrightarrow n \in \operatorname{dom} f'$, and suppose $n + 1 \in \operatorname{dom} f$. Then $n \in \operatorname{dom} f$, so $n \in \operatorname{dom} f'$, and $f(n) = f'(n)$. Hence

$$(n, f'(n)) = (n, f(n)) \in \operatorname{dom} G,$$

and so $n + 1 \in \operatorname{dom} f'$. Thus $n + 1 \in \operatorname{dom} f \Rightarrow n + 1 \in \operatorname{dom} f'$, and vice versa. So $\operatorname{dom} f = \operatorname{dom} f'$. This completes the proof.

Denotational semantics involves the definition of a collection of semantic functions by mutual recursion over the syntactic structure of phrases of the object language. The partial recursion theorem generalizes to this case in exactly the same way as does the usual recursion theorem for total functions. The proof differs from that above in the complexity of its detail, but not in its essence.

2.4.5 *Generalized mu-terms*

The third and final extension to the Z notation is a generalized form of the μ-term which gives something like the effect of a let-definition in an ISWIM-like programming language. An example of such an generalized μ-term is

$$\mu\, x : \mathsf{N} \mid x * x = 16 \bullet x + 3.$$

This has value 7, because there is just one value of x, namely $x = 4$, which satisfies the predicate $x * x = 16$, and with this value of x, the term $x + 3$ takes the value 7. The μ-terms

$$\mu\, x : \mathsf{N} \mid x * x = 15 \bullet x + 3,$$
$$\mu\, x : \mathsf{N} \mid x * x = x \bullet x + 3,$$
$$\mu\, x : \mathsf{N} \mid x * x = 9 \bullet 12/(x - 3)$$

are all undefined, the first because there is no value of x satisfying the predicate, the second because there is more than one, and the third because the term $12/(x-3)$ is undefined at the value of x which satisfies the predicate, namely 3.

If the final term is omitted, the default is a tuple made up of the variables of the declaration, so

$$(\mu\, x, y : \mathsf{N} \mid x = 3 \wedge y = 4)$$
$$= (\mu\, x, y : \mathsf{N} \mid x = 3 \wedge y = 4 \bullet (x, y))$$
$$= (3, 4).$$

This default convention means that the usual form of the μ-term can be regarded as a special case of the extended form.

2.5 The language of schemas

The concepts explained above will be used in chapter 3 to give a full denotational semantics of the Z notation, but it is good to begin here with the semantics of a less ambitious fragment, in which previously defined schemas may be combined with the operations of the schema calculus.

We shall consider a little language of schemas, in which schema expressions can be combined with the operations of conjunction, disjunction and projection:

$$SEXP ::= \cdots$$
$$| \quad SEXP \wedge SEXP$$
$$| \quad SEXP \vee SEXP$$
$$| \quad SEXP \upharpoonright SEXP$$
$$| \quad \cdots$$

The meaning of a schema expression is defined by a semantic function *sexp* which, given an environment of schema definitions, maps schema expressions to varieties—the details of environments are irrelevant here, but are covered in subsection 3.2.2.

> *sexp* : *ENV* → *SEXP* ↛ *VARIETY*
>
> $\cdots$
>
> *sexp* $\rho \, [se_1 \wedge se_2] \cong combine(sexp \, \rho \, [se_1], sexp \, \rho \, [se_2])$
>
> $\cdots$

The meaning of the conjunction of two schema expressions is obtained by putting together the varieties corresponding to the two arguments using the auxiliary function *combine*. This joins the signatures using the function *join*, which identifies the common variables, and the class of models is described in terms of the function *restrict*. The models of the conjoined schema are those which satisfy, in a certain sense, the axioms of both the arguments.

> *combine* : *VARIETY* × *VARIETY* ↛ *VARIETY*
>
> $combine(\theta VARIETY_1, \theta VARIETY_2) \cong$
> $\mu \, VARIETY' \, |$
> $\quad sig' \cong join(sig_1, sig_2) \wedge$
> $\quad models' =$
> $\quad\quad \{ M : Struct(sig') \, |$
> $\quad\quad\quad restrict \, sig_1 \, M \in models_1 \wedge$
> $\quad\quad\quad restrict \, sig_2 \, M \in models_2 \, \}.$

This definition bears a striking resemblance to the definition of parallel composition in CSP (Hoare, 1985) if we regard signatures and models as analogous to alphabets and traces respectively:

$$\alpha(P \parallel Q) = \alpha P \cup \alpha Q$$
$$traces(P \parallel Q) =$$
$$\{\, t \in \alpha(P \parallel Q)^* \mid t \restriction \alpha P \in traces(P) \land t \restriction \alpha Q \in traces(Q)\,\}.$$

The disjunction of two schemas A and B is defined similarly: the signatures are still joined in the same way, but the models are those which satisfy either the axioms of A or those of B:

> $\ldots$
>
> $sexp\ \rho\,\llbracket se_1 \lor se_2 \rrbracket \cong disjoin(sexp\ \rho\,\llbracket se_1 \rrbracket, sexp\ \rho\,\llbracket se_2 \rrbracket)$
>
> $\ldots$

The operation *disjoin* is defined exactly like *combine*, except that the *models* component of the result is given by

$$models' =$$
$$\{\, M : Struct(sig') \mid$$
$$restrict\ sig_1\ M \in models_1 \lor$$
$$restrict\ sig_2\ M \in models_2 \,\}.$$

The semantics of schema projection is defined in terms of an operation *project*:

> $\ldots$
>
> $sexp\ \rho\,\llbracket se_1 \restriction se_2 \rrbracket \cong project(sexp\ \rho\,\llbracket se_1 \rrbracket, sexp\ \rho\,\llbracket se_2 \rrbracket)$
>
> $\ldots$

The standard definition of $A \restriction B$ hides those components of A which are not in the signature of B. It is required that the signature of A includes the signature of B, and the axioms of B are ignored. The models in the result are those structures for the signature of B which can be obtained by restriction from a model of A.

> $project : VARIETY \times VARIETY \nrightarrow VARIETY$
>
> ---
>
> $project(\theta\,VARIETY_1, \theta\,VARIETY_2) \cong$
> $\quad \mu\,VARIETY' \mid$
> $\qquad sig_2\ \textbf{subsig}\ sig_1 \land$
> $\qquad sig' = sig_2 \land$
> $\qquad models' = restrict\ sig_2\,\llparenthesis models_1 \rrparenthesis.$

An alternative definition might require the models in the result to be models for B as well: this effect would be obtained by setting

$models' = models_2 \cap restrict\ sig_2\ (models_1)$.

These examples show how the theory of varieties can be applied to the semantics of some simple Z constructs. Of course, for a full semantics of Z it is necessary to describe the environments which record definitions of schemas and the process by which generic schemas can be instantiated with particular types, as well as the mathematical sublanguage in which the axiom parts of schemas are expressed, and these are the main tasks of Chapter 3.

CHAPTER THREE

THE SEMANTICS OF Z

This chapter contains a variety-based denotational semantics for a simple but powerful specification language closely similar to the Z notation as it is used today. In this language, specifications may introduce named schemas, global given-set names and global constants specified by axioms. Schemas may have generic parameters, and there are notations for taking an instance of a generic schema and for combining schemas with the operations of the schema calculus.

Z has evolved over several years, so the notation used in particular published specifications may be different from that described here. Also, the abstract syntax for the language uses keywords rather than the more suggestive boxes for defining schemas. This helps to make the semantic equations more concise, but the same semantics can be used with the more usual concrete syntax based on boxes.

The chapter begins with a brief summary of the specification language which is the subject of the formal semantics. The presentation of the formal semantics itself begins in section 3.2 with a description of the *environments* which record the schemas and global variables introduced in a specification. Level numbers are used to distinguish identifiers declared at different lexical levels, and this provides the means to model the Z scope rules. The next few sections then define the semantic functions, linking the abstract syntax with the semantic domains. Each section deals with a different syntactic class taken from the syntax summary in subsection 3.1.1. The index of definitions at the back of the book provides cross-references between different parts of the semantics.

One important feature of the Z notation is not present in the specification language of this chapter. This is the facility for making global generic definitions, used extensively in the standard library or tool-kit of mathematical definitions: the concept of relation, for example, is generic in the sets from which the domain and range are drawn. Formalizing the semantics of this Z feature presents some difficulties, so its description delayed until chapter 4.

3.1 Language summary

What follows is a summary of the specification language whose formal semantics is given in this chapter. The syntax of the language has been simplified to make the semantics more concise. One simplification is the use of keywords instead of boxes, and another is the omission of infix function and relation symbols; these are just a more readable way to write certain function applications and membership predicates. A specification consists of a sequence of definitions, which are of three kinds.

Definitions of global given-set names. These introduce a number of given-set names global to the whole specification: typically, these given sets will be sets assumed known in the specification, but whose details are not important. An example might be the sets of valid file-names and of data blocks in a filing system.

Example.

> **given** *FILENAME, BLOCK* .

In the usual syntax of Z, these names are introduced by writing them in square brackets:

> [*FILENAME, BLOCK*].

Definitions of global variables. These introduce variables which are global to the whole specification, and allow axioms which constrain their values. The axioms need not determine the values of the variables exactly, but may leave some 'looseness': this allows objects to be named whose details are not needed in the specification; it also allows requirements to be captured accurately without unduly constraining the implementation. Many definitions of global variables, however, just introduce convenient abbreviations.

Examples.

> let
>
> $$f : \mathsf{N} \times \mathsf{N} \to \mathsf{N}$$
>
> |
>
> $$\forall\, n, m : \mathsf{N} \bullet f(n, m) = 10 * n + m$$
>
> end.

> let
>
> $$encode : CHAR \rightarrowtail \mathsf{N};$$
> $$decode : \mathsf{N} \twoheadrightarrow CHAR$$
>
> |
>
> $$decode = encode^{-1}$$
>
> end.

In the usual syntax, definitions of global variables are written with a vertical bar on the left, but without bars above and below, for example:

$$f : \mathsf{N} \times \mathsf{N} \to \mathsf{N}$$
$$\forall\, n, m : \mathsf{N} \bullet f(n, m) = 10 * n + m.$$

Definitions of schemas. Each of these introduces a new schema name, which may have generic parameters. The right-hand side of the definition may be simply the text of the schema, or it may be a schema expression built up from already-defined schema names.

Examples.

> let $POOL[RESOURCE] =$ **schema**
> $$inuse, avail : \mathsf{P}\ RESOURCE$$
>
> |
>
> $$inuse \cap avail = \varnothing$$
>
> end.

> let $LOOKUP = (LOOKUP1 \wedge Ok) \vee ErrNotFound.$

In the usual syntax, definitions like the first one are given by attaching the schema name to a box containing the text:

$$
\begin{array}{|l|}
\hline
\;POOL[RESOURCE] \underline{\hspace{3cm}} \\
\;inuse, avail : \mathsf{P}\ RESOURCE \\
\hline
\;inuse \cap avail = \varnothing \\
\hline
\end{array}
$$

Definitions of one schema in terms of others use the definition sign $\hat{=}$:

$$LOOKUP \; \hat{=} \; (LOOKUP1 \wedge Ok) \vee ErrNotFound.$$

A *schema designator* is an applied occurrence of a schema name. As well as the schema name itself, it may contain a decoration to be applied uniformly to all the components of the schema, and some actual generic parameters. Schema designators may be used in schema expressions, and also in *declarations*, the parts of schema bodies which introduce variables. The axiom part of a schema body is a *predicate*, and these may be built up in any of the usual ways from the most basic predicates, which are equations and membership predicates between *terms*.

3.1.1 *Syntax summary*

Specifications

$$
\begin{aligned}
SPEC ::= \; &\textbf{given } IDENT, \ldots, IDENT \\
| \; &\textbf{let } SCHEMA \textbf{ end} \\
| \; &\textbf{let } WORD[IDENT, \ldots, IDENT] = SEXP \\
| \; &SPEC \textbf{ in } SPEC.
\end{aligned}
$$

Schema expressions

$$
\begin{aligned}
SEXP ::= \; &\textbf{schema } SCHEMA \textbf{ end} \\
| \; &SDES \\
| \; &\neg \; SEXP \\
| \; &SEXP \wedge SEXP \\
| \; &SEXP \vee SEXP \\
| \; &SEXP \Rightarrow SEXP \\
| \; &SEXP \upharpoonright SEXP \\
| \; &SEXP \setminus (IDENT, \ldots, IDENT) \\
| \; &\exists \, SCHEMA \bullet SEXP \\
| \; &\forall \, SCHEMA \bullet SEXP.
\end{aligned}
$$

Schema designators

$$SDES ::= WORD \, DECOR[TERM, \ldots, TERM].$$

Schema bodies

$$SCHEMA ::= DECL \mid PRED.$$

Declarations

$DECL ::= IDENT : TERM$
$\quad\quad\quad | \quad SDES$
$\quad\quad\quad | \quad DECL\,;\,DECL.$

Predicates

$PRED ::= TERM = TERM$
$\quad\quad\quad | \quad TERM \in TERM$
$\quad\quad\quad | \quad \textbf{true}$
$\quad\quad\quad | \quad \textbf{false}$
$\quad\quad\quad | \quad \neg\,PRED$
$\quad\quad\quad | \quad PRED \wedge PRED$
$\quad\quad\quad | \quad PRED \vee PRED$
$\quad\quad\quad | \quad PRED \Rightarrow PRED$
$\quad\quad\quad | \quad \exists\,SCHEMA \bullet PRED$
$\quad\quad\quad | \quad \forall\,SCHEMA \bullet PRED.$

Terms

$TERM ::= IDENT$	– identifier.
$\quad | \quad \varnothing[TERM]$	– null set.
$\quad | \quad \{TERM,\ldots,TERM\}$	– extensive set.
$\quad | \quad \{SCHEMA \bullet TERM\}$	– comprehension.
$\quad | \quad SDES$	– schema designator.
$\quad | \quad \textbf{P}\,TERM$	– power-set.
$\quad | \quad (TERM,\ldots,TERM)$	– tuple.
$\quad | \quad TERM \times \cdots \times TERM$	– Cartesian product.
$\quad | \quad \theta\,WORD\,DECOR$	– θ-term.
$\quad | \quad TERM\,.\,IDENT$	– selection.
$\quad | \quad TERM(TERM)$	– function application.
$\quad | \quad \lambda\,SCHEMA \bullet TERM$	– λ-term.
$\quad | \quad \mu\,SCHEMA \bullet TERM$	– μ-term.

Identifiers

$IDENT ::= WORD\,DECOR$

Primitive classes

$WORD$ – undecorated identifiers.
$DECOR$ – decoration.

3.2   Modelling scope

Nested scopes are introduced into Z specifications when global variables are defined and then used in the definition of schemas, and by use of the quantifiers ∀ and ∃ and the quantifier-like constructs beginning λ, μ and {. Because the same identifier may be introduced in several nested declarations, we need some way of describing which declaration is linked with each applied occurrence of an identifier.

A solution is to work with signatures which contain not the identifiers themselves, but 'names' consisting of an identifier tagged with the lexical level of its declaration. A function mapping identifiers to the corresponding names in a particular signature can then be defined quite simply, and the semantics of nested constructs is simplified, because signatures are always extended by adding names at a new lexical level, rather than replacing hidden names with the names that hide them, and this means that the old signature is always a sub-signature of the new one. Models for the old signature can be obtained simply by restricting models for the new one.

The global given-set names and global variables of a specification together form the signature of a global variety: the models component of this variety captures the information in the axiom parts of global variable definitions. Each schema is represented by a variety whose signature contains *both* the generic parameters and components of the schema *and* the global given-set names and variables to which it may refer. Local and global variables with the same identifier are distinguished in the signature by tagging them with level numbers. As an example, the specification

> **let** $x, y : \mathbb{N} \mid x + y = 10$ **in**
> **let** $FOO =$ **schema** $y : \mathbb{N} \mid y > x$ **end**.

has two global variables x and y, and in the models of the global variety, x any y may take as values any pair of natural numbers which sum to 10. The schema FOO is represented by a variety with three variables x^0, y^0, and y^1, where the superscripts are level numbers. The models of this variety assign natural numbers to these three variables in such a way that x^0 and y^0 sum to 10, and y^1 is larger than x^0. This device of level numbers allows the relationship between local and global variables to be captured even when some local variables hide global variables with the same identifiers.

3.2.1   *Names*

A *name* is an identifier tagged with a level number. The outermost part of a specification is level 0, the variables of a schema are at level 1, and so on:

higher numbers are needed e.g. for quantifiers. The operation *Tag* of tagging is a bijection because each name determines uniquely the identifier and level number. For convenience, a curried variant *tag* of the tagging function is introduced also.

$[IDENT, NAME]$

$LEVEL \mathrel{\widehat=} \mathbb{N}$

$$
\begin{array}{|l}
Tag : LEVEL \times IDENT \rightarrowtail NAME \\
tag : LEVEL \rightarrow IDENT \rightarrow NAME \\
\hline
tag\ k\ x = Tag(k, x).
\end{array}
$$

Two rules are used to determine the name to which any applied occurrence of an identifier refers:

1. Names at higher levels hide those at lower levels.

2. Variables hide given-set names at the same level.

If an identifier x is looked up in some level k of an alphabet S, the corresponding name will be *tag k x*, provided that this is in S.

$$
\begin{array}{|l}
lookup : \mathbb{P}\,NAME \times LEVEL \rightarrow IDENT \rightarrowtail NAME \\
\hline
lookup(S, k) = (tag\ k) \rhd S.
\end{array}
$$

Now a function *one_level* can be defined which looks for an identifier at a single level in a signature. It returns a value of type *NAMEREF* which says whether the name is a given-set name or a variable. Rule 2 is followed here in that the function for looking up variables overrides the one for given-set names.

$$NAMEREF ::= gref \langle\!\langle NAME \rangle\!\rangle \mid vref \langle\!\langle NAME \rangle\!\rangle$$

$$
\begin{array}{|l}
one\_level : SIG \times LEVEL \rightarrow IDENT \rightarrowtail NAMEREF \\
\hline
one\_level(\Sigma, k) = \\
\quad gref \circ (lookup(\Sigma.given, k)) \oplus vref \circ (lookup(\Sigma.vars, k)).
\end{array}
$$

Finally, the function *find* looks for an identifier in all levels of a signature up to a given level k. It is defined by recursion on k, and rule 1 is followed by making higher levels override lower ones.

$$find : SIG \times LEVEL \rightarrow IDENT \nrightarrow NAMEREF$$

$$find(\Sigma, 0) = one\_level(\Sigma, 0)$$
$$find(\Sigma, k + 1) = find(\Sigma, k) \oplus one\_level(\Sigma, k + 1).$$

Identifiers themselves cannot be regarded as atomic because of the notation for systematic renaming or decoration. Instead, they are regarded as consisting of an (atomic) *word* followed by a *decoration*. A word and a decoration can be combined with the bijection *paint* to give an identifier. Decorations can be combined by the binary operation $\diamond$ of *juxtaposition*, and there is a function *decorate* which applies a decoration to identifiers by juxtaposing it with the decoration already present. Juxtaposition is associative, and there is a decoration *blank* which acts as a left and right identity for juxtaposition.

$$[WORD, DECOR]$$

$$paint : WORD \times DECOR \rightarrowtail IDENT$$
$$\_\diamond\_ : DECOR \times DECOR \rightarrow DECOR$$
$$blank : DECOR$$
$$decorate : DECOR \rightarrow IDENT \rightarrow IDENT$$

$$a \diamond (b \diamond c) = (a \diamond b) \diamond c$$
$$a \diamond blank = blank \diamond a = a$$
$$decorate\ b\ (paint(w, a)) = paint(w, a \diamond b).$$

3.2.2 Environments

Fragments of Z text may refer to given-set names and variables introduced in a previous piece of specification, as well as previously defined schema names. In order to make sense of the text, therefore, we must supply an environment containing the definitions of these names.

The global given-set names and variables are combined to make a global signature, and a class of models for this signature allows the specified relationship among these names to be recorded. This gives a variety *global*, which is made part of the environment. There is also dictionary *sdict* mapping each previously defined schema name to its definition, an object of type *SMEANING*:

$$
\begin{array}{|l}
\_ENV \underline{\hspace{8cm}} \\
\quad global : VARIETY \\
\quad sdict : WORD \twoheadrightarrow SMEANING \\
\hline
\quad \forall\, sm : \operatorname{ran} sdict \bullet \\
\qquad basis(sm.local.sig) \text{ subsig } global.sig \\
\end{array}
$$

The meaning recorded for a schema name in the environment consists of a variety *local* and a sequence *fparam* which records the order of the formal generic parameters:

$$
\begin{array}{|l}
\_SMEANING \underline{\hspace{7cm}} \\
\quad local : VARIETY \\
\quad fparam : \operatorname{seq} IDENT \\
\hline
\quad fparam^{-1} \in locids(local.sig.given) \rightarrowtail \mathbb{N} \\
\quad local.sig.given \cup local.sig.vars \subseteq basename \cup localname \\
\quad local.sig \in \operatorname{dom} basis \\
\end{array}
$$

The signature of the variety *local* contains not only the local variables or components of the schema, but also the global variables to which the schema may refer. As well as the formal generic parameters, it contains the global given-set names which may be mentioned in the schema. The local and global names are distinguished by tagging global names at level 0, and local names at level 1. The axiom part of the schema may describe a relationship between the local and global variables, and the presence of both allows this relationship to be recorded in the *models* component of *local*.

The global variables mentioned in a schema must be among the ones declared in the global part of the specification; this requirement is formalized in the axiom for *ENV*. The given-set names and variable names in the definition must all be at level 0 (*basename*) or at level 1 (*localname*), and the names at level 0 must be a well-formed signature in their own right, which is to say that the types of global variables must be formed from global given-set names alone.

The function *locids* in the above definition gives the set of identifiers at level 1 in an alphabet of names, and *localname* is the set of all such names:

$$
\begin{array}{|l}
\hline
locids : \mathbb{P}\ NAME \rightarrow \mathbb{P}\ IDENT \\
localname : \mathbb{P}\ NAME \\
\hline
locids(S) = (tag\ 1)^{-1}(\!|S|\!) \\
localname = \operatorname{ran}(tag\ 1). \\
\hline
\end{array}
$$

The global part (at level 0) of a signature is given by the function *basis*; a signature has a well-formed global part iff the types of the variables at level 0 contain only given-set names at level 0.

$$
\begin{array}{|l}
\hline
basis : SIG \rightarrowtail SIG \\
basename : \mathbb{P}\ NAME \\
\hline
basis = \\
\quad \lambda\ SIG \mid type(\!|basename|\!) \subseteq Type(basename) \bullet \\
\quad \mu\ SIG' \mid \\
\qquad given' = basename \cap given\ \wedge \\
\qquad vars' = basename \cap vars\ \wedge \\
\qquad type' = basename \lhd type \\
basename = \operatorname{ran}(tag\ 0). \\
\hline
\end{array}
$$

3.2.3 Operations on environments

Conceptually, all specifications start with the empty environment *arid*:

$$
\begin{array}{|l}
\hline
arid : ENV \\
\hline
arid = \\
\quad \mu\ ENV \mid \\
\qquad global.sig = null\_sig\ \wedge \\
\qquad global.models = Struct(global.sig)\ \wedge \\
\qquad sdict = \varnothing. \\
\hline
\end{array}
$$

In practice, specifications assume certain standard definitions, and these can be made part of the initial environment of the specification.

Environments are extended by declaring new variables and given-set names, and defining new schemas. The commonest operation is to add new variables and given-set names with axioms relating them, and this is modelled by the function *enrich*:

$$
\begin{array}{|l}
\hline
enrich : ENV \times VARIETY \rightarrowtail ENV \\
\hline
enrich = \\
\quad \lambda\, \rho : ENV;\ V : VARIETY \mid \rho.global \text{ subvar } V \bullet \\
\quad \mu\, \rho' : ENV \mid \\
\qquad \rho'.global = V \wedge \\
\qquad \rho'.sdict = \rho.sdict. \\
\hline
\end{array}
$$

The new variables and given set names are part of a new variety V, the *models* part of which relates the new names to those in the environment ρ. The global part of ρ must be a sub-variety of V: this corresponds to the fact that declarations add variables and never take them away, and new axioms add to the consequences of a specification, but never invalidate any properties which held without them. Any theorem which can be proved from some set of axioms can also be proved when extra axioms are added—the new axioms can just be ignored, and the same proof establishes the theorem.

The other way of extending an environment is by adding a new schema:

$$
\begin{array}{|l}
\hline
add\_schema : ENV \times WORD \times SMEANING \rightarrowtail ENV \\
\hline
add\_schema = \\
\quad \lambda\, \rho : ENV;\ w : WORD;\ sm : SMEANING \mid \\
\qquad w \notin \operatorname{dom} \rho.sdict \wedge \\
\qquad basis(sm.local.sig) \text{ subsig } \rho.global.sig \bullet \\
\quad \mu\, \rho' : ENV \mid \\
\qquad \rho'.global = \rho.global \wedge \\
\qquad \rho'.sdict = \rho.sdict \cup \{w \mapsto sm\}. \\
\hline
\end{array}
$$

This just extends the schema dictionary with the new definition.

3.3   Declarations

Declarations introduce new variables and associate them with types. There are two elementary kinds of declaration: one of these introduces a single variable, the type being given by a set-valued term, and the other introduces all the variables of a schema by means of a schema designator (*SDES*)—the semantics of these is given in section 3.7. Declarations may be combined with ';', and such a composite declaration introduces all the variables introduced by either of its arguments: variables introduced by both arguments must have the same type in both.

$$DECL ::= IDENT : TERM$$
$$| \quad SDES$$
$$| \quad DECL; DECL.$$

As a convenience, the declaration

$$x, y, z : X$$

is defined to be syntactic sugar for the composite declaration

$$x : X; y : X; z : X.$$

The main purpose of a declaration is to establish a signature, but the terms giving the types of variables and the schemas which are included may also contain information given by axioms. This information is preserved by making the result of the semantic function a variety: the models in this variety are the ones which satisfy the axioms.

$$decl : ENV \rightarrow LEVEL \rightarrow DECL \nrightarrow VARIETY$$

$$decl \, \rho \, k \, [\![x : t]\!] \cong$$
$$\quad \mu \, tt : TMEANING \mid tt \cong term \, \rho \, k \, [\![t]\!] \bullet$$
$$\quad \mu \, a : TYPE \mid tt.type = powerT \, a \bullet$$
$$\quad new\_var(\rho.global, tag \, k \, x, a, tt.eval)$$
$$decl \, \rho \, k \, [\![sd]\!] \cong sdes \, \rho \, k \, [\![sd]\!]$$
$$decl \, \rho \, k \, [\![d_1; d_2]\!] \cong combine(decl \, \rho \, k \, [\![d_1]\!], decl \, \rho \, k \, [\![d_2]\!]).$$

A simple variable declaration introduces one new variable, and the function *new_var* constructs the variety which results from this. As an example, in the declaration

$$n : 1 .. 10,$$

the term $1 .. 10$ has type $\mathbb{P} \, \mathbb{N}$, so the type of n will be $\mathbb{N}$—this is the type a in the semantic equation above. The evaluation function (see section 3.4) for the term $1 .. 10$ will be a constant function which always yields (the W representation of) the set $\{1, 2, \ldots, 10\}$, so n will always have one of the values $1, 2, \ldots, 10$.

A number of restrictions must be obeyed by a variable declaration. The variable being declared must not already be present in the signature, and its proposed type must be formed from the right alphabet. The term after the colon in a variable declaration must be defined in every model for the global part of the specification: this places a proof-obligation on the author of a specification, but ensures that the range of a variable is always well-defined.

The variety which results from the declaration contains all the global variables in addition to the new variable; each model of this variety can be obtained by extending a model of the global variety with a value of the new variable chosen from the specified set.

$$
\begin{array}{l}
new\_var : VARIETY \times NAME \times TYPE \\
\qquad\qquad\qquad\qquad \times (STRUCT \nrightarrow W) \nrightarrow VARIETY \\
\hline
new\_var = \\
\quad \lambda\, VARIETY_0;\ lhs : NAME;\ rhs : TYPE; \\
\qquad\qquad\qquad\qquad\qquad eval : STRUCT \nrightarrow W \mid \\
\quad lhs \notin sig_0.vars \wedge \\
\quad a \in Type(sig_0.given) \wedge \\
\quad \mathrm{dom}\ eval = models_0 \wedge \\
\quad (\forall\, M : models_0 \bullet eval(M) \sqsubseteq Carrier\ M.gset\ a) \bullet \\
\mu\, VARIETY \mid \\
\quad sig.given = sig_0.given \wedge \\
\quad sig.vars = sig_0.vars \cup \{lhs\} \wedge \\
\quad sig.type = sig_0.type \cup \{lhs \mapsto rhs\} \wedge \\
\quad models = \\
\qquad \{\, M : Struct(sig) \mid \\
\qquad\qquad restrict\ sig_0\ M \in models_0 \wedge \\
\qquad\qquad M.val(lhs) \in eval(restrict\ sig_0\ M)\,\}.
\end{array}
$$

The meaning of a composite declaration $d_1;\ d_2$ is obtained by combining the meanings of d_1 and d_2 with the function *combine* described in section 2.5. Because of the properties of the operation *join* on signatures, and the properties of *restrict* noted in section 2.3, the operation *combine* is idempotent, commutative and associative, and the declaration-combining operator ';' shares these properties. We can also provide an identity element for ';': it is the empty declaration **empty** which introduces no variables:

$$DECL ::= \ldots \mid \mathbf{empty}$$

$$
\begin{array}{l}
\hline
\quad \ldots \\
\hline
\quad decl\, \rho\, k\ [\mathbf{empty}] \cong \rho.global.
\end{array}
$$

3.4 Terms

There are several ways of forming terms in Z:

$$
\begin{array}{lll}
TERM ::= & IDENT & - \text{identifier.} \\
| & \varnothing[TERM] & - \text{null set.} \\
| & \{TERM, \ldots, TERM\} & - \text{extensive set.} \\
| & \{SCHEMA \bullet TERM\} & - \text{comprehension*.} \\
| & SDES & - \text{schema designator.} \\
| & \mathbf{P}\ TERM & - \text{power-set.} \\
| & (TERM, \ldots, TERM) & - \text{tuple.} \\
| & TERM \times \cdots \times TERM & - \text{Cartesian product.} \\
| & \theta\ WORD\ DECOR & - \theta\text{-term.} \\
| & TERM . IDENT & - \text{selection.} \\
| & TERM(TERM) & - \text{function application.} \\
| & \lambda\ SCHEMA \bullet TERM & - \lambda\text{-term.} \\
| & \mu\ SCHEMA \bullet TERM & - \mu\text{-term*.} \\
\end{array}
$$

In the two forms marked with an asterisk, the term following the dot may be omitted: the default is the 'characteristic tuple' of the schema before the dot, which is determined by its declaration part. If this has the simple form

$$x : t,$$

then the characteristic tuple is just the variable x. If it is a schema designator,

$$A'[t_1, \ldots, t_n],$$

the characteristic tuple is the θ-term $\theta A'$. Finally, if the declaration has the form

$$d_1;\ d_2;\ \ldots;\ d_n,$$

with $n \geq 2$, and $d_1, d_2, \ldots, d_n$ take the two simple forms above, then the characteristic tuple is

$$(t_1, t_2, \ldots, t_n),$$

where for $1 \leq i \leq n$, t_i is the characteristic tuple of d_i. Characteristic tuples are also involved in the semantics of λ-terms, and the notation $char\_tuple\ [s]$ is used for the characteristic tuple of a schema s. Strictly speaking, the notion of characteristic tuple violates the principle of referential transparency; this is discussed in section 4.2. The meaning of a term is a pair consisting of a type and a partial function giving the value of the term in models of its environment:

```
┌─ TMEANING ──────────────────────────────────
│ type : TYPE
│ eval : STRUCT ↛ W
└──────────────────────────────────────────────
```

The semantic function for terms is

$$term : ENV \rightarrow LEVEL \rightarrow TERM \nrightarrow TMEANING$$

but instead of defining it by semantic equations, we shall use 'inference systems' which allow the meaning of a term to be deduced. The first of these deals with the type part of the meaning, and the second with the evaluation function. This idea of describing the well-typing and evaluation of expressions by inference systems is an important part of the 'structured operational semantics' approach of (Plotkin, 1981), and is also applied in (Burstall & Lampson, 1984).

The inference system for types operates on *type-ascriptions* of the form

$$\rho, k \vdash t :: a,$$

where ρ is an environment, k is a level number, t is a term, and a is a type. This formula should be read "in environment ρ, t has type a". The antecedents of the inference rules are usually just type-ascriptions, but sometimes references to other parts of the semantics occur when terms contain embedded declarations, schema bodies, and so on.

The inference system depends only on the finite signature part of the environment, and not on the information supplied by axioms in the specification, which is recorded in the potentially infinite models part. Also, there is exactly one inference rule which allows type-ascriptions to be deduced for each kind of term, so the structure of the derivation of the type of a term is completely determined by the structure of the term itself. In short, the typing of terms is decidable; the inference rules might be transcribed directly into a rule-based programming language and, together with a coding of the signature parts of the rest of the semantics, this would give a type-checker for Z specifications.

The second inference system deals with the evaluation-function part of the meaning of a term, and is less like the familiar inference systems of logic than the first one, in that its operations are far from being effectively given. It operates on *evaluations* of the form

$$\rho, k, M \vdash t \Rightarrow u,$$

where ρ, k and t are as before, M is a structure in $\rho.global.models$, and u is an element of the world of sets W. This formula should be read "in environment ρ, the model M gives t the value u".

Many of the rules use operations from the world-of-sets specification to manipulate the values u in evaluations, and it is these which make the system non-effective: this so-called inference system is really just a way of defining a complicated function in a notation which allows pattern-matching, but the style of presentation makes comparison with the type-inference rules easier. In some places, type-ascriptions appear among the antecedents of a rule of inference, and these are to be derived using rules from the first inference system.

The complete set of well-typing rules is given in subsection 3.4.1 and the evaluation rules are in subsection 3.4.2; only a few example rules are explained here. One of the simplest pairs of rules deals with tuples. The well-typing rule is

$$\frac{\rho, k \vdash t_i :: a_i \quad (1 \leq i \leq n)}{\rho, k \vdash (t_1, \ldots, t_n) :: a_1 \times \cdots \times a_n.}$$

This says that if e.g. r, s, t are well-typed terms with types A, B, C, then (r, s, t) is also well-typed, and its type is $A \times B \times C$. The corresponding evaluation rule is

$$\frac{\rho, k, M \vdash t_i \Rightarrow u_i \quad (1 \leq i \leq n)}{\rho, k, M \vdash (t_1, \ldots, t_n) \Rightarrow tuple\langle u_1, \ldots, u_n \rangle.}$$

This just says that if r, s, t have the values 3, 4, 5, then the tuple-term (r, s, t) has as value (the W representation of) the tuple $(3, 4, 5)$. So the evaluation rule makes a link between the syntactic construction of tuple-terms and the operation of tupling in the world of sets.

Two important properties of terms are that the type of a term contains only given-set names from its environment, and that the value of a term is always an element of its type. These properties can be proved by induction on the structure of terms. More formally, the properties are that if

$$\rho, k \vdash t :: a$$

and

$$\rho, k, M \vdash t \Rrightarrow u,$$

then

(i) $a \in Type(\rho.global.sig.given)$, and

(ii) $u \sqsubseteq Carrier\ M.gset\ a$.

In the case of tuple-terms, we suppose that (i) and (ii) hold of t_i, a_i and u_i for $1 \le i \le n$, and show that they hold of t, a and u, where

$$t = [\![(t_1, \ldots, t_n)]\!],$$
$$a = [\![a_1 \times \cdots \times a_n]\!] = tuple\,T\,\langle a_1, \ldots, a_n \rangle,$$
$$u = tuple\,\langle u_1, \ldots, u_n \rangle.$$

(i) follows because

$$names(a)$$
$$= names(tuple\,T\,\langle a_1, \ldots, a_n \rangle)$$
$$= \bigcup names(\!\mathrm{ran}\,\langle a_1, \ldots, a_n \rangle\!)$$
$$= names(a_1) \cup \cdots \cup names(a_n),$$

and $names(a_i) \subseteq \rho.global.sig.given$ for $0 \le i \le n$ by hypothesis. For (ii), let $S_i = Carrier\ M.gset\ a_i$ for $1 \le i \le n$. Then

$$Carrier\ M.gset\ a$$
$$= Carrier\ M.gset\,(tuple\,T\,\langle a_1, \ldots, a_n \rangle)$$
$$= cproduct(map\,(Carrier\ M.gset)\,\langle a_1, \ldots, a_n \rangle)$$
$$= cproduct\,\langle S_1, \ldots, S_n \rangle.$$

But by hypothesis, $u_i \sqsubseteq S_i$ for $1 \le i \le n$, so by the axiom defining $cproduct$,

$$u = tuple\,\langle u_1, \ldots, u_n \rangle \sqsubseteq cproduct\,\langle S_1, \ldots, S_n \rangle$$

as required. The proofs for the other kinds of term are along similar lines.

So the value of a term t in an environment ρ is always an element of the type of t, and

$$term\,\rho\,k\,[\![t]\!] \in Tmeaning(\rho.global)$$

where the function *Tmeaning* is defined by:

> *Tmeaning* : *VARIETY* $\twoheadrightarrow$ **P** *TMEANING*
>
> ---
>
> *Tmeaning*(*V*) =
>   { *TMEANING* |
>   *type* $\in$ *Type*(*V.sig.given*) $\wedge$
>   dom *eval* $\subseteq$ *V.models* $\wedge$
>   ($\forall M$: dom *eval* $\bullet$ *eval*(M) $\in$ *Carrier M.gset type*) }.

A slightly more complicated pair of rules covers Cartesian product terms; they allow the Cartesian product construction, originally a way of constructing types, to be used on set-valued terms in general. The well-typing rule is as follows:

$$\frac{\rho, k \;\vdash\; t_i :: \mathbf{P}\; a_i \quad (1 \le i \le n)}{\rho, k \;\vdash\; t_1 \times \cdots \times t_n :: \mathbf{P}(a_1 \times \cdots \times a_n).}$$

The Cartesian product operation must operate on set-valued terms, so the antecedent of this rule requires the arguments to have power-set types. The result also has a power-set type: it is a set of tuples formed from elements of the arguments. The corresponding evaluation rule is

$$\frac{\rho, k, M \;\vdash\; t_i \Rightarrow u_i \quad (1 \le i \le n)}{\rho, k, M \;\vdash\; t_1 \times \cdots \times t_n \Rightarrow cproduct \,\langle u_1, \ldots, u_n \rangle.}$$

This just makes the link with the Cartesian product operation in the world of sets. The property that the value of a Cartesian product term is an element of its type follows from the monotonicity of type constructors as discussed in section 2.2.

As a concrete example, the term $1 .. 3$ has type **P** $\mathbb{N}$—it denotes a set of natural numbers, as does the term $2 .. 4$, so the well-typing rule for Cartesian product terms allows us to deduce that the term $(1 .. 3) \times (2 .. 4)$ has type $\mathbf{P}(\mathbb{N} \times \mathbb{N})$—it is a set of pairs of natural numbers. The axiom defining the *cproduct* operation says that each member of this set has the form (a, b) where $a \in 1 .. 3$ and $b \in 2 .. 4$.

A θ-term constructs a binding from the values of the components of a schema: if A is a schema with components p and q, then θA is a binding containing the values of p and q. The term $\theta A'$ is a binding in which p takes the value of p' and q takes the value of q'. The well-typing rule for θ-terms is

$$\frac{\begin{array}{l} locids((\rho.sdict\ A).local.sig.vars) \cong \{x_1, \ldots, x_n\} \\ \rho, k\ \vdash\ x_i(') :: a_i \quad (1 \le i \le n) \end{array}}{\rho, k\ \vdash\ \theta A(') :: \langle\!\langle x_1 : a_1;\ \ldots;\ x_n : a_n \rangle\!\rangle}$$

This gives the type of a θ-term $\theta A(')$ where A is a schema name and $(')$ symbolizes a possible decoration. To find the type of this term, we first find out the identifiers of the components of A, say $x_1, \ldots, x_n$, and find the types of $x_1('), \ldots, x_n(')$, the decorated counterparts of these, in the environment. The type of $\theta A(')$ is then a schema product type with the *undecorated* components $x_1, \ldots, x_n$ having these types. The reason for the schema product type to have undecorated components is that we want to write equations such as

$$\theta STATE = \theta STATE',$$

and for this to be possible, the terms $\theta STATE$ and $\theta STATE'$ must have the same type. It is not enough to allow equations between terms of types equal 'up to decoration', for we also want the set-comprehension

$$\{\ STATE;\ STATE'\ |\ Pred\ \},$$

which is equivalent to

$$\{\ STATE;\ STATE'\ |\ Pred \bullet (\theta STATE, \theta STATE')\ \},$$

to define a homogeneous relation on states, and this will only happen if $\theta STATE$ and $\theta STATE'$ have the same type.

The evaluation rule just makes a binding from the values of the variables in the environment:

$$\frac{\begin{array}{l} locids((\rho.sdict\ A).local.sig.vars) \cong \{x_1, \ldots, x_n\} \\ \rho, k, M\ \vdash\ x_i(') \Rightarrow u_i \quad (1 \le i \le n) \end{array}}{\rho, k, M\ \vdash\ \theta A(') \Rightarrow binding\ \{x_1 \mapsto u_1, \ldots, x_n \mapsto u_n\}.}$$

The operation of selection also involves schema product types. The well-typing rule is simple enough:

$$\frac{\rho, k\ \vdash\ t :: \langle\!\langle x_1 : a_1;\ \ldots;\ x_n : a_n \rangle\!\rangle}{\rho, k\ \vdash\ t.x_j :: a_j \quad (1 \le j \le n).}$$

The evaluation rule, however, needs a type-ascription as antecedent. This represents an interaction between well-typing and evaluation, and is necessary because we assume only that binding formation is injective for named collections *with the same alphabet*.

$$\frac{\rho, k \; \vdash \; t :: \langle\!\langle x_1 : a_1; \; \ldots; x_n : a_n \rangle\!\rangle}{\rho, k, M \; \vdash \; t \Rightarrow binding \; \{x_1 \mapsto u_1, \ldots, x_n \mapsto u_n\}}$$

$$\rho, k, M \; \vdash \; t.x_j \Rightarrow u_j \quad (1 \leq j \leq n).$$

Another interaction between well-typing and evaluation occurs in the case of set-comprehension terms, where the type of a term is used to find a set bounding its range of values. The well-typing and evaluation rules are as follows:

$$\frac{\rho_1 \cong enrich(\rho, schema \; \rho \, k \; [\![s]\!])}{\rho_1, k+1 \; \vdash \; t :: a}$$
$$\rho, k \; \vdash \; \{ s \bullet t \} :: \mathsf{P} \, a,$$

$$\frac{\rho_1 \cong enrich(\rho, schema \; \rho \, k \; [\![s]\!])}{\begin{array}{l} \rho_1, k+1 \; \vdash \; t :: a \\ \mathrm{dom} \; uu = extend \; (\rho.global.sig, \rho_1.global) \, M \\ \forall M' : \mathrm{dom} \; uu \bullet (\, \rho_1, k+1, M' \; \vdash \; t \Rightarrow uu(M')\,) \end{array}}$$
$$\rho, k, M \; \vdash \; \{ s \bullet t \} \Rightarrow filter(Carrier \; M.gset \; a, \mathrm{ran} \; uu).$$

In the set-comprehension term $\{ s \bullet t \}$, the schema body s introduces variables which may be used in the term t. This is reflected in the well-typing rule by taking the type of t in an environment ρ_1 enriched with the variables of s. The type of the comprehension is the power-type of this type: for example, if the type of x is N, then the term $x + x$ also has type N, so the set-comprehension $\{ x : \mathsf{N} \bullet x + x \}$ has type $\mathsf{P} \, \mathsf{N}$: it is a *set* of natural numbers, namely the even ones. If the term t is omitted, it is taken by default to be the characteristic tuple of s, as noted above, so the type of $\{ x, y : \mathsf{N} \mid x > y \}$ is the same as that of $\{ x, y : \mathsf{N} \mid x > y \bullet (x, y) \}$, that is, $\mathsf{P}(\mathsf{N} \times \mathsf{N})$.

The evaluation rule uses an auxiliary function *extend* which is a kind of inverse for *restrict*: if Σ is a sub-signature of $V.sig$, and $M \in Struct(\Sigma)$, then $extend \, (\Sigma, V) \, M$ is the set of structures in $V.models$ which give M on restriction:

$$extend : SIG \times VARIETY \twoheadrightarrow STRUCT \twoheadrightarrow \mathbf{P} \, STRUCT$$

$$
\begin{aligned}
extend = {}& \\
& \lambda \, \Sigma : SIG; \; V : VARIETY \mid \Sigma \; subsig \; V.sig \bullet \\
& \quad \lambda \, M : Struct(\Sigma) \bullet \\
& \qquad \{ \, M' : V.models \mid restrict \, \Sigma \, M' = M \, \}.
\end{aligned}
$$

The antecedents of the evaluation rule for set-comprehension terms demand that the term t be well-typed with some type a, and that t have a value in every extension of the model M, these values being given by a mapping uu. The value of the set-comprehension term is then the range of uu, and this is known to be represented in the world of sets because it is a subset of the carrier of a.

3.4.1 *Well-typing rules*

Identifiers

$$find \, (\rho.global.sig, k) \, x \cong vref(v)$$
$$\rho.global.sig.type(v) = a$$

$$\rule{5cm}{0.4pt}$$

$$\rho, k \vdash x :: a$$

$$find \, (\rho.global.sig, k) \, x \cong gref(G)$$

$$\rule{5cm}{0.4pt}$$

$$\rho, k \vdash x :: \mathbf{P} \, G$$

Null set

$$\rho, k \vdash t :: \mathbf{P} \, a$$

$$\rule{4cm}{0.4pt}$$

$$\rho, k \vdash \varnothing[t] :: \mathbf{P} \, a$$

Extensive set

$$\rho, k \vdash t_i :: a \quad (1 \leq i \leq n)$$

$$\rule{5cm}{0.4pt}$$

$$\rho, k \vdash \{t_1, \ldots, t_n\} :: \mathbf{P} \, a$$

Comprehension

$$\rho_1 \cong enrich(\rho, schema \, \rho \, k \, [s])$$
$$\rho_1, k{+}1 \vdash t :: a$$

$$\rule{5cm}{0.4pt}$$

$$\rho, k \vdash \{ s \bullet t \} :: \mathbf{P} \, a$$

Schema designator

$$\frac{\rho, k \;\vdash\; \{\, sd \bullet \theta sd \,\} :: a}{\rho, k \;\vdash\; sd :: a}$$

Power-set

$$\frac{\rho, k \;\vdash\; t :: \mathbf{P}\, a}{\rho, k \;\vdash\; \mathbf{P}\, t :: \mathbf{P}(\mathbf{P}\, a)}$$

Tuple

$$\frac{\rho, k \;\vdash\; t_i :: a_i \quad (1 \le i \le n)}{\rho, k \;\vdash\; (t_1, \ldots, t_n) :: a_1 \times \cdots \times a_n}$$

Cartesian product

$$\frac{\rho, k \;\vdash\; t_i :: \mathbf{P}\, a_i \quad (1 \le i \le n)}{\rho, k \;\vdash\; t_1 \times \cdots \times t_n :: \mathbf{P}(a_1 \times \cdots \times a_n)}$$

θ-term

$$\frac{\begin{array}{c} locids((\rho.sdict\, A).local.sig.vars) \cong \{x_1, \ldots, x_n\} \\ \rho, k \;\vdash\; x_i(') :: a_i \quad (1 \le i \le n) \end{array}}{\rho, k \;\vdash\; \theta A(') :: \langle\!\langle x_1 : a_1; \; \ldots; \; x_n : a_n \rangle\!\rangle}$$

Selection

$$\frac{\rho, k \;\vdash\; t :: \langle\!\langle x_1 : a_1; \; \ldots; \; x_n : a_n \rangle\!\rangle}{\rho, k \;\vdash\; t.x_j :: a_j \quad (1 \le j \le n)}$$

Function application

$$\frac{\begin{array}{c} \rho, k \;\vdash\; t_1 :: \mathbf{P}(a \times a') \\ \rho, k \;\vdash\; t_2 :: a \end{array}}{\rho, k \;\vdash\; t_1(t_2) :: a'}$$

λ-term

$$t_1 = char\_tuple\,[s]$$
$$\rho, k \;\vdash\; \{\, s \bullet (t_1, t) \,\} :: a$$

$$\rho, k \;\vdash\; \lambda\, s \bullet t :: a$$

μ-term

$$\rho, k \;\vdash\; \{\, s \bullet t \,\} :: \mathbf{P}\, a$$

$$\rho, k \;\vdash\; \mu\, s \bullet t :: a$$

3.4.2   *Evaluation rules*

Identifiers

$$find\,(\rho.global.sig, k)\, x \cong vref(v)$$
$$M.val(v) = u$$

$$\rho, k, M \;\vdash\; x \Rrightarrow u$$

$$find\,(\rho.global.sig, k)\, x \cong gref(G)$$
$$M.gset(G) = u$$

$$\rho, k, M \;\vdash\; x \Rrightarrow u$$

Null set

$$\rho, k, M \;\vdash\; \varnothing[t] \Rrightarrow null$$

Extensive set

$$\rho, k, M \;\vdash\; t_i \Rrightarrow u_i \quad (1 \leq i \leq n)$$

$$\rho, k, M \;\vdash\; \{t_1, \ldots, t_n\} \Rrightarrow rep\,\{u_1, \ldots, u_n\}$$

Comprehension

$$\rho_1 \cong enrich(\rho, schema\, \rho\, k\, [s])$$
$$\rho_1, k{+}1 \;\vdash\; t :: a$$
$$dom\, uu = extend\,(\rho.global.sig, \rho_1.global)\, M$$
$$\forall M' : dom\, uu \bullet (\rho_1, k{+}1, M' \;\vdash\; t \Rrightarrow uu(M'))$$

$$\rho, k, M \;\vdash\; \{\, s \bullet t \,\} \Rrightarrow filter(Carrier\, M.gset\, a, ran\, uu)$$

Schema designator

$$\frac{\rho, k, M \vdash \{ sd \bullet \theta sd \} \Rrightarrow u}{\rho, k, M \vdash sd \Rrightarrow u}$$

Power-set

$$\frac{\rho, k, M \vdash t \Rrightarrow u}{\rho, k, M \vdash \mathbf{P}\, t \Rrightarrow power(u)}$$

Tuple

$$\frac{\rho, k, M \vdash t_i \Rrightarrow u_i \quad (1 \leq i \leq n)}{\rho, k, M \vdash (t_1, \ldots, t_n) \Rrightarrow tuple\, \langle u_1, \ldots, u_n \rangle}$$

Cartesian product

$$\frac{\rho, k, M \vdash t_i \Rrightarrow u_i \quad (1 \leq i \leq n)}{\rho, k, M \vdash t_1 \times \cdots \times t_n \Rrightarrow cproduct\, \langle u_1, \ldots, u_n \rangle}$$

θ-term

$$\frac{\begin{array}{l} locids((\rho.sdict\, A).local.sig.vars) \cong \{x_1, \ldots, x_n\} \\ \rho, k, M \vdash x_i(') \Rrightarrow u_i \quad (1 \leq i \leq n) \end{array}}{\rho, k, M \vdash \theta A(') \Rrightarrow binding\, \{x_1 \mapsto u_1, \ldots, x_n \mapsto u_n\}}$$

Selection

$$\frac{\begin{array}{l} \rho, k \vdash t :: \langle\!| x_1 : a_1; \ldots; x_n : a_n |\!\rangle \\ \rho, k, M \vdash t \Rrightarrow binding\, \{x_1 \mapsto u_1, \ldots, x_n \mapsto u_n\} \end{array}}{\rho, k, M \vdash t.x_j \Rrightarrow u_j \quad (1 \leq j \leq n)}$$

Function application

$$\frac{\begin{array}{l} \rho, k, M \vdash t_1 \Rrightarrow u \\ \rho, k, M \vdash t_2 \Rrightarrow v \\ tuple\, \langle v, v' \rangle \in u \\ \forall w : W \bullet tuple\, \langle v, w \rangle \in u \Rightarrow w = v' \end{array}}{\rho, k, M \vdash t_1(t_2) \Rrightarrow v'}$$

λ-term

$$\frac{\begin{array}{l} t_1 = char\_tuple \, [s] \\ \rho, k, M \; \vdash \; \{\, s \bullet (t_1, t)\,\} \Rrightarrow u \end{array}}{\rho, k, M \; \vdash \; \lambda s \bullet t \Rrightarrow u}$$

μ-term

$$\frac{\rho, k, M \; \vdash \; \{\, s \bullet t \,\} \Rrightarrow rep\,\{u\}}{\rho, k, M \; \vdash \; \mu s \bullet t \Rrightarrow u}$$

3.5   Predicates

Elementary predicates are of three kinds: equality between terms of the same type, the membership predicate between a term of type a and another of type $\mathbf{P}\,a$, and the logical constants **true** and **false**. These may be combined with all the usual logical connectives, and quantified with 'for all' and 'there exists':

$$
\begin{aligned}
PRED ::= \; & TERM = TERM \\
        | \; & TERM \in TERM \\
        | \; & \mathbf{true} \\
        | \; & \mathbf{false} \\
        | \; & \neg\, PRED \\
        | \; & PRED \wedge PRED \\
        | \; & PRED \vee PRED \\
        | \; & PRED \Rightarrow PRED \\
        | \; & \exists\, SCHEMA \bullet PRED \\
        | \; & \forall\, SCHEMA \bullet PRED.
\end{aligned}
$$

The other kinds of predicates—infix relation symbols, unique quantifiers, and so on—can be defined as syntactic sugar for combinations of these few forms. Of course, these forms are not themselves independent: for example, '$\Rightarrow$' can be defined in terms of '$\neg$' and '$\vee$':

$$P \Rightarrow Q \;\;\widehat{=}\;\; \neg\, P \vee Q.$$

A predicate is modelled in the semantics by the set of structures which satisfy it. For the moment, we deal with partially defined terms by fixing a semantics for the equality sign which makes

$$t_1 = t_2$$

true if t_1 and t_2 are both defined with values equal, and false otherwise, and fixing a similar semantics for the membership sign. These issues will be discussed further in chapter 4. The rest of the semantics of predicates is a completely classical truth-definition. The logical connectives are made to correspond to elementary set-theoretic operations on the sets of structures; $\wedge$ to intersection, $\vee$ to union, and so on. The semantics of quantifiers is given in terms of the functions *restrict* and *extend*, which link the environment with the result of enriching it with the bound variables of the quantifier.

$$pred : ENV \rightarrow LEVEL \rightarrow PRED \rightarrow \mathbb{P}\, STRUCT$$

$pred\, \rho\, k\, [t_1 = t_2] \cong$
$\quad \mu\, tt_1, tt_2 : TMEANING \mid$
$\qquad tt_1 \cong term\, \rho\, k\, [t_1] \wedge$
$\qquad tt_2 \cong term\, \rho\, k\, [t_2] \wedge$
$\qquad tt_1.type = tt_2.type \bullet$
$\quad \{\, M : \rho.global.models \mid$
$\qquad\quad M \in (dom\, tt_1.eval) \cap (dom\, tt_2.eval) \wedge$
$\qquad\quad tt_1.eval(M) = tt_2.eval(M) \,\}$

$pred\, \rho\, k\, [t_1 \in t_2] \cong$
$\quad \mu\, tt_1, tt_2 : TMEANING \mid$
$\qquad tt_1 \cong term\, \rho\, k\, [t_1] \wedge$
$\qquad tt_2 \cong term\, \rho\, k\, [t_2] \wedge$
$\qquad powerT\, tt_1.type = tt_2.type \bullet$
$\quad \{\, M : \rho.global.models \mid$
$\qquad\quad M \in (dom\, tt_1.eval) \cap (dom\, tt_2.eval) \wedge$
$\qquad\quad tt_1.eval(M) \sqsubseteq tt_2.eval(M) \,\}$

$pred\, \rho\, k\, [\mathbf{true}] \cong \rho.global.models$

$pred\, \rho\, k\, [\mathbf{false}] \cong \varnothing$

$pred\, \rho\, k\, [\neg\, p] \cong \rho.global.models \setminus pred\, \rho\, k\, [p]$

$pred\, \rho k [p_1 \wedge p_2] \cong pred\, \rho\, k\, [p_1] \cap pred\, \rho\, k\, [p_2]$

$pred\, \rho\, k\, [p_1 \vee p_2] \cong pred\, \rho\, k\, [p_1] \cup pred\, \rho\, k\, [p_2]$

$pred\, \rho\, k\, [p_1 \Rightarrow p_2] \cong$
$\quad \rho.global.models \setminus (pred\, \rho\, k\, [p_1] \setminus pred\, \rho\, k\, [p_2])$

$$pred\ \rho\ k\ [\exists\ s\ \bullet\ p] \cong$$
$$\mu\ \rho_1 : ENV \mid \rho_1 \cong enrich(\rho, schema\ \rho\ k\ [s]) \bullet$$
$$restrict\ \rho.global.sig\ (pred\ \rho_1\ (k{+}1)\ [p])$$
$$pred\ \rho\ k\ [\forall\ s\ \bullet\ p] \cong$$
$$\mu\ \rho_1 : ENV \mid \rho_1 \cong enrich(\rho, schema\ \rho\ k\ [s]) \bullet$$
$$\{\ M : \rho.global.models \mid$$
$$extend\ (\rho.global.sig, \rho_1.global)\ M \subseteq pred\ \rho_1\ (k{+}1)\ [p]\ \}.$$

3.6   Schema bodies

A schema body consists of a declaration constrained by a predicate. Schema
bodies may appear in many places in a Z specification: after quantifiers,
after λ, and so on, as well as in the definition of schemas. The meaning of
a schema body is a variety—it is the one which results from selecting those
models of the declaration which also satisfy the predicate:

$$SCHEMA ::= DECL \mid PRED$$

$$schema : ENV \rightarrow LEVEL \rightarrow SCHEMA \nrightarrow VARIETY$$

$$schema\ \rho\ k\ [d \mid p] \cong$$
$$\mu\ \rho_1 : ENV \mid \rho_1 \cong enrich(\rho, decl\ \rho\ k\ [d]) \bullet$$
$$\mu\ VARIETY \mid$$
$$sig = \rho_1.global.sig \wedge$$
$$models \cong pred\ \rho_1\ (k{+}1)\ [p].$$

The predicate part of a schema body may be omitted in any context; the
default is the logical constant **true**. Also, a list of predicates may be written
in place of a single predicate: this is equivalent to the conjunction of the
predicates.

3.7   Schema designators

A schema designator is an applied occurrence of a schema name. The components of the named schema can be subjected to systematic decoration,
and actual parameters are substituted for the formal generic parameters
of the definition. So, syntactically, a schema designator consists of a word

naming the schema, a decoration—possibly blank—to be applied to the component names, and a list of set-valued terms which are the actual generic parameters:

$$SDES ::= WORD \: DECOR\,[TERM,\ldots,TERM].$$

The meaning of a schema designator is a variety: it has all the given-set names and variables of the global part of the environment, together with the local variables of the schema. The model class represents information from three sources: first, the global part of the specification, second, the axioms of the schema itself, and third, the actual parameters of the schema designator. I shall give the semantics in three stages, dealing first with schema designators without parameters, then with ones which have types as parameters, and finally with the most general case, where any set-valued terms can appear as parameters.

The simplest kind of schema designator refers to a schema without formal parameters—its meaning is found by looking up the name of the schema in the schema dictionary part of the environment, then retagging the local variables at the current level and applying the decoration. The resulting variety contains the local variables of the schema and those global variables which were in scope when it was defined, so the result must be combined with the global part of the environment to add the variables declared since then, and information from later axioms.

$$SDES1 ::= WORD \: DECOR$$

$$sdes1 : ENV \to LEVEL \to SDES1 \nrightarrow VARIETY$$

$$sdes1\,\rho\,k\,\lfloor w\ q\rceil \cong$$
$$\quad \mu\,sm : SMEANING \mid$$
$$\qquad sm \cong \rho.sdict(w) \land$$
$$\qquad \#sm.fparam = 0 \bullet$$
$$\quad combine(\rho.global,\ retag\,(q,k)\ sm.local).$$

The *retag* operation renames local variables, which are at level 1, and converts them to level k. The given-set names are simply retagged, but the variables themselves are also decorated.

$$retag : DECOR \times LEVEL \to VARIETY \nrightarrow VARIETY$$

$$retag\,(q,k) =$$
$$\quad rename\,(id\ basename \cup (tag\ k) \circ (tag\ 1)^{-1},$$
$$\qquad id\ basename \cup (tag\ k) \circ (decorate\ q) \circ (tag\ 1)^{-1}).$$

The next stage in sophistication is to allow types as actual parameters. The semantics can be given by first deriving a variety—in the same way as just described—which contains the formal parameters as well as the global given-set names and global and local variables. Models of this variety are then selected in which the values of the formal parameters are equal to the carriers of the actual parameter types, and the formal parameters are hidden using *restrict*. The actual parameters are incorporated in two ways: they are substituted for the formal parameters in the types of variables, and the sets assigned to formal parameters in a model are constrained to be the same as the carriers of the actual parameters.

$$SDES2 ::= WORD\ DECOR\ [TYPE, \ldots, TYPE]$$

$$sdes2 : ENV \to LEVEL \to SDES2 \nrightarrow VARIETY$$

$$sdes2\ \rho\ k\ [\![w\ q\ [a_1, \ldots, a_n]\!]\!] \cong$$
$$\mu\ sm : SMEANING;\ formal : \text{seq}\ NAME\ |$$
$$\quad sm \cong \rho.sdict(w) \land$$
$$\quad formal = (tag\ k) \circ sm.fparam \land$$
$$\quad \#formal = n \bullet$$
$$\mu\ actual : \text{seq}\ TYPE\ |$$
$$\quad actual = \langle a_1, \ldots, a_n \rangle \land$$
$$\quad \text{ran}\ actual \subseteq Type(\rho.global.sig.given) \bullet$$
$$\mu\ V_1 : VARIETY\ |$$
$$\quad V_1 \cong combine(\rho.global, retag\ (q, k)\ sm.local) \bullet$$
$$\mu\ VARIETY\ |$$
$$\quad sig.given = \rho.global.sig.given \land$$
$$\quad sig.vars = V_1.sig.vars \land$$
$$\quad sig.type =$$
$$\quad\quad (tsubst\ (givenT \oplus (actual \circ formal^{-1}))) \circ V_1.sig.type \land$$
$$\quad models =$$
$$\quad\quad \{\ M : V_1.models\ |$$
$$\quad\quad\quad M.gset \circ formal = (Carrier\ M.gset) \circ actual \bullet$$
$$\quad\quad\quad restrict\ sig\ M\ \}.$$

Here is a small example to illustrate the definition. Suppose A is the schema of section 2.3,

$$\begin{array}{|l}
\hline
\_A[X, Y] \underline{\hspace{6cm}} \\
p : X \\
q : X \times Y \\
\hline
\exists\, y : Y \bullet q = (p, y) \\
\hline
\end{array}$$

Consider the schema designator $A[\mathsf{N}, \mathsf{P}\,\mathsf{N}]$. This has a signature in which p has type N and q has type $\mathsf{N} \times \mathsf{P}\,\mathsf{N}$: these types are the result of substituting N for X and $\mathsf{P}\,\mathsf{N}$ for Y in the original signature. To find the models, we take those models of A in which X has value N and Y has value $\mathsf{P}\,\mathsf{N}$, then forget X and Y. Because the values of p and q lay in the carriers of their types originally, and the values of X and Y matched the carriers of the actual parameters, the values of p and q also agree with the new signature.

The most general form of schema designator allows any set-valued term to be used as an actual parameter. The types of these parameters are used to determine the types of variables in the resulting variety, and an additional constraint is placed on models that the values of the formal parameters and those of the actual parameter terms be equal. The semantic equation uses a function *instantiate* which is also used in the semantics of generic definitions (see section 4.1).

$$\begin{array}{|l}
sdes : ENV \rightarrow LEVEL \rightarrow SDES \twoheadrightarrow VARIETY \\
\hline
sdes\, \rho\, k\, [\![w\, q\, [t_1, \ldots, t_n]]\!] \cong \\
\quad instantiate(\rho.global, k, \rho.sdict(w), q, map\,(term\,\rho\,k)\,\langle t_1, \ldots, t_n \rangle).
\end{array}$$

The *instantiate* operation first extracts type and value information from the parameter terms, giving a sequence *actype* of types and a function *actval* from models of the environment to sequences of values. For simplicity, it is assumed that the parameter terms are always defined. The parameter terms must also have type $\mathsf{P}\,a$ for some type a, and *actype* is the result of stripping off the 'P'.

Next, a variety V_1 is derived by combining varieties from the current environment and from the schema. This variety is then modified by substituting the types in *actype* for the formal parameters, and constraining the values of the formal parameters to be as given by *actval*, before hiding the formal parameters.

$instantiate : VARIETY \times LEVEL \times SMEANING \times DECOR$
$\qquad\qquad\qquad \times \text{seq } TMEANING \nrightarrow VARIETY$

$instantiate(V_0, k, sm, q, tt) \cong$
$\quad \mu \, formal : \text{seq } NAME \mid$
$\qquad formal = (tag \, k) \circ sm.fparam \wedge$
$\qquad \#formal = \#tt \wedge$
$\qquad (\forall \, tm : \text{ran } tt \bullet$
$\qquad\qquad tm \in Tmeaning(V_0) \wedge tm.type \in \text{ran } powerT \wedge$
$\qquad\qquad \text{dom } tm.eval = V_0.models) \bullet$
$\quad \mu \, actype : \text{seq } TYPE; \; actval : STRUCT \nrightarrow \text{seq } W \mid$
$\qquad powerT \circ actype = (\lambda \, TMEANING \bullet type) \circ tt \wedge$
$\qquad actval =$
$\qquad\qquad (\lambda \, M : V_0.models \bullet (\lambda \, TMEANING \bullet eval(M)) \circ tt) \bullet$
$\quad \mu \, V_1 : VARIETY \mid$
$\qquad V_1 \cong combine(V_0, retag \, (q, k) \, sm.local) \bullet$
$\quad \mu \, VARIETY \mid$
$\qquad sig.given = V_0.sig.given \wedge$
$\qquad sig.vars = V_1.sig.vars \wedge$
$\qquad sig.type =$
$\qquad\qquad (tsubst \, (givenT \oplus (actype \circ formal^{-1}))) \circ V_1.sig.type \wedge$
$\qquad models =$
$\qquad\qquad \{ \, M : V_1.models \mid$
$\qquad\qquad\qquad M.gset \circ formal = actval(restrict \, V_0.sig \, M) \bullet$
$\qquad\qquad\qquad restrict \, sig \, M \, \}.$

As an example, consider the schema designator $A[1 \mathbin{..} 2, 6 \mathbin{..} 7]$. Here the actual parameters both have type $\mathbb{P}\,\mathbb{N}$, and the signature of the result gives p and q types $\mathbb{N}$ and $\mathbb{N} \times \mathbb{N}$ respectively: $\mathbb{N}$ has been substituted for both X and Y, the '$\mathbb{P}$' having been stripped. Not all structures for this signature will do, however, even if they satisfy the axiom of A: in addition, the value of p must be in $1 \mathbin{..} 2$, and that of q must be in $(1 \mathbin{..} 2) \times (6 \mathbin{..} 7)$. The models of the result are those obtained by restricting models of the variety V_1 in which X and Y take values $\{1, 2\}$ and $\{6, 7\}$ respectively.

It is possible to prove that the models in the result of *instantiate* do in fact agree with the signature: that the value of each variable lies in the carrier of its type. If M' is any model in the result, then $M' = restrict \, sig \, M$ for some $M : V_1.models$ with

$\qquad M.gset \circ formal = actval \, M_0,$

where $M_0 = (restrict\ V_0.sig\ M)$. The sequence tt of actual parameters is drawn from $Tmeaning(V_0)$, so for each $i : 1 .. \#tt$,

$M.gset\,(formal\ i)$

$\quad = (actval\ M_0)\ i$

$\quad = (tt\ i).eval\ M_0$

$\quad \sqsubseteq Carrier\ M_0.gset\,(tt\ i).type$

$\quad = Carrier\ M.gset\,(powerT\,(actype\ i))$

$\quad = power\,(Carrier\ M.gset\,(actype\ i)).$

So $M.gset\,(formal\ i) \sqsubseteq Carrier\ M.gset\,(actype\ i)$. The types of variables in the result are obtained by applying the substitution

$$tm = givenT \oplus (actype \circ formal^{-1}).$$

Consider any given-set name $G : V_1.sig.given$. If $G \in \operatorname{ran} formal$ then $tm\ G = actype\,(formal^{-1}\ G)$, so

$Carrier\ M.gset\,(tm\ G)$

$\quad = Carrier\ M.gset\,(actype\,(formal^{-1}\ G))$

$\quad \sqsupseteq M.gset\,(formal\,(formal^{-1}\ G))$

$\quad = M.gset\ G.$

If $G \notin \operatorname{ran} formal$ then $tm\ G = givenT\ G$, so

$Carrier\ M.gset\,(tm\ G)$

$\quad = Carrier\ M.gset\,(givenT\ G)$

$\quad = M.gset\ G.$

In either case, $M.gset\ G \sqsubseteq Carrier\ M.gset\,(tm\ G)$. By monotonicity of the type constructors, for any $t : Type(V_1.sig.given)$,

$Carrier\ M.gset\ t$

$\quad \sqsubseteq Carrier\,((Carrier\ M.gset) \circ tm)\ t$

$\quad = Carrier\ M.gset\,(tsubst\ tm\ t).$

So for any variable $v : sig.vars$,

$M'.val\ v$
$\quad = M.val\ v$
$\quad \sqsubseteq Carrier\ M.gset\ (V_1.sig.type\ v)$
$\quad \sqsubseteq Carrier\ M.gset\ (tsubst\ tm\ (V_1.sig.type\ v))$
$\quad = Carrier\ M.gset\ (sig.type\ v)$
$\quad = Carrier\ M'.gset\ (sig.type\ v).$

Thus $M'.val\ v \sqsubseteq Carrier\ M'.gset\ (sig.type\ v)$.

3.8   Schema expressions

Schema expressions are built up from schema bodies and schema designators by various combining operators:

$SEXP ::=$ **schema** $SCHEMA$ **end**
$\quad | \quad SDES$
$\quad | \quad \neg\ SEXP$
$\quad | \quad SEXP \wedge SEXP$
$\quad | \quad SEXP \vee SEXP$
$\quad | \quad SEXP \Rightarrow SEXP$
$\quad | \quad SEXP \upharpoonright SEXP$
$\quad | \quad SEXP \setminus (IDENT, \ldots, IDENT)$
$\quad | \quad \exists\, SCHEMA \bullet SEXP$
$\quad | \quad \forall\, SCHEMA \bullet SEXP.$

Some of these operators were defined in the example of section 2.5, and we adopt the same definitions here after modifying them to deal with nested scopes. Others are new, and their semantics is defined in terms of some auxiliary functions described later in this section.

$sexp : ENV \rightarrow LEVEL \rightarrow SEXP \nrightarrow VARIETY$

$sexp\ \rho\ k\ [\textbf{schema}\ s\ \textbf{end}] \cong schema\ \rho\ k\ [s]$

$sexp\ \rho\ k\ [sd] \cong sdes\ \rho\ k\ [sd]$

$sexp\ \rho\ k\ [\neg\ se] \cong combine(\rho.global, negate(sexp\ \rho\ k\ [se]))$

$sexp\ \rho\ k\ [se_1 \wedge se_2] \cong combine(sexp\ \rho\ k\ [se_1], sexp\ \rho\ k\ [se_2])$

$sexp\ \rho\ k\ [se_1 \vee se_2] \cong disjoin(sexp\ \rho\ k\ [se_1], sexp\ \rho\ k\ [se_2])$

$sexp\ \rho\ k\ [se_1 \Rightarrow se_2] \cong$
$\qquad combine(\rho.global, imply(sexp\ \rho\ k\ [se_1], sexp\ \rho\ k\ [se_2]))$

$sexp\ \rho\ k\ [\![se_1 \upharpoonright se_2]\!] \cong project(sexp\ \rho\ k\ [\![se_1]\!], sexp\ \rho\ k\ [\![se_2]\!])$

$sexp\ \rho\ k\ [\![se \setminus (x_1, \ldots, x_n)]\!] \cong$
  $hide(sexp\ \rho\ k\ [\![se]\!], tag\ k\ (\!\{x_1, \ldots, x_n\}\!))$

$sexp\ \rho\ k\ [\![\exists\ s \bullet se]\!] \cong$
  $\mu\ V_1 : VARIETY\ |\ V_1 \cong schema\ \rho\ k\ [\![s]\!] \bullet$
  $hide(combine(V_1, sexp\ \rho\ k\ [\![se]\!]), V_1.sig.vars \setminus \rho.global.sig.vars)$

$sexp\ \rho\ k\ [\![\forall\ s \bullet se]\!] \cong$
  $\mu\ V_1 : VARIETY\ |\ V_1 \cong schema\ \rho\ k\ [\![s]\!] \bullet$
  $univ(imply(V_1, sexp\ \rho\ k\ [\![se]\!]), V_1.sig.vars \setminus \rho.global.sig.vars).$

The most basic kinds of schema expression are schema bodies, which give the text of the schema, and schema designators, which refer to a previously named schema. The semantics of these constructs is given in sections 3.6 and 3.7 respectively.

Schema expressions can be combined with any of the connectives of the propositional calculus, and here we show '$\neg$', '$\wedge$', '$\vee$', and '$\Rightarrow$' as examples. The negation operator takes the complement of the class of models of its argument:

$negate : VARIETY \rightarrow VARIETY$

$negate(\theta VARIETY) =$
  $\mu\ VARIETY'\ |$
  $sig' = sig\ \wedge$
  $models' = Struct(sig) \setminus models.$

The result of this operation must be combined in the semantic equation with the global part of the environment, because we are interested only in models which fail to satisfy the axioms of the schema whilst still satisfying the global axioms of the specification.

The definitions of '$\wedge$' and '$\vee$' follow those given in section 2.5; the nesting of scopes is handled automatically by the scheme of tagging variable names. The variety which results must contain the global part of the environment as a sub-variety, but this is assured by the properties of *combine* and *disjoin*. Implication is defined in terms of the function *imply*, consistency with the global part of the specification again being obtained by using *combine*.

$imply : VARIETY \times VARIETY \nrightarrow VARIETY$

$imply(V_1, V_2) \cong disjoin(negate(V_1), V_2).$

Next we come to various hiding operations. The projection operator '$\upharpoonright$' is as described in section 2.5, and the operator '$\backslash$', which allows particular variables to be hidden, is defined in terms of the function *hide*:

$hide : VARIETY \times \mathbf{P} \, NAME \rightarrow VARIETY$
$hide\_sig : SIG \times \mathbf{P} \, NAME \rightarrow SIG$

$hide(\theta VARIETY, S) =$
$\quad \mu VARIETY' \mid$
$\qquad sig' = hide\_sig(sig, S) \wedge$
$\qquad models' = restrict \, sig' \, (\!models\!)$
$hide\_sig(\theta SIG, S) =$
$\quad \mu SIG' \mid$
$\qquad sig'.given = sig.given \wedge$
$\qquad sig'.vars = sig.vars \setminus S \wedge$
$\qquad sig'.type = sig'.vars \lhd sig.type.$

The existential quantifier operation is a variant of hiding in which the axiom part of a schema constrains the models of a schema expression and its local variables are hidden: this is rather like removing the variables from the signature of the schema expression and existentially quantifying them in the axiom part.

The universal quantifier likewise corresponds to removing the variables of a schema from the signature of a schema expression and universally quantifying them in the axiom part. The classical equivalence between the universal and existential quantifiers continues to hold in the schema calculus:

$$\forall s \bullet se \; \hat{=} \; \neg \, (\exists s \bullet \neg \, se),$$

where the quantifiers and negation signs have their interpretation as schema operations. However, we give here an explicit definition of the universal quantifier in terms of a function *univ*:

$univ : VARIETY \times VARIETY \times \mathbf{P} \, NAME \nrightarrow VARIETY$

$univ(\theta VARIETY, S) \cong$
$\quad \mu VARIETY' \mid$
$\qquad sig' = hide\_sig(sig, S) \wedge$
$\qquad models' = \{ \, M' : Struct(sig') \mid$
$\qquad\qquad \{ \, M : Struct(sig) \mid restrict \, sig' \, M = M' \, \} \subseteq models \, \}.$

3.9 Specifications

The smallest specification is a definition, which may introduce some global given-set names, introduce some global variables with some axioms, or define a new schema. Definitions may be joined with **in**, and then the names introduced by the first are added to the environment before the second is considered.

$$SPEC ::= \textbf{given } IDENT, \ldots, IDENT$$
$$| \textbf{ let } SCHEMA \textbf{ end}$$
$$| \textbf{ let } WORD[IDENT, \ldots, IDENT] = SEXP$$
$$| SPEC \textbf{ in } SPEC.$$

A specification is evaluated in an initial environment—this might contain the definitions of the standard mathematical tool-kit, and it produces a new environment, enriched with the new objects defined in the specification.

$spec : ENV \rightarrow SPEC \twoheadrightarrow ENV$

$spec\ \rho\ [\textbf{given } x_1, \ldots, x_n] \cong$
    $enrich(\rho, new\_givens(\rho.global, tag\ 0\ (\{x_1, \ldots, x_n\})))$

$spec\ \rho\ [\textbf{let } s\ \textbf{end}] \cong enrich(\rho, schema\ \rho\ 0\ [s])$

$spec\ \rho\ [\textbf{let } w[x_1, \ldots, x_n] = se] \cong$
    $\mu\ \rho_1 : ENV\ |\ \rho_1 \cong$
            $enrich(\rho, new\_givens(\rho.global, tag\ 1\ (\{x_1, \ldots, x_n\}))) \bullet$
    $\mu\ sm : SMEANING\ |$
            $sm.local \cong sexp\ \rho_1\ 1\ [se] \wedge$
            $sm.fparam = \langle x_1, \ldots, x_n \rangle \bullet$
        $add\_schema(\rho, w, sm)$

$spec\ \rho\ [z_1\ \textbf{in}\ z_2] \cong \mu\ \rho_1 : ENV\ |\ \rho_1 \cong spec\ \rho\ [z_1] \bullet spec\ \rho_1\ [z_2].$

The declaration of global given-set names or global variables simply enriches the global variety of the environment. Because of the semantics of declarations and the definition of *new_givens* (see below), it is meaningless to declare the same global variable or given-set name twice. A schema definition adds a new schema name to the dictionary. The formal generic parameters may be used in the defining schema expression, and their order is preserved in the *fparam* sequence for matching with actual parameters in schema designators.

The operation *new_givens* adds new given-set names to a variety in much the same way as *new_var* (section 3.3). The definition is slightly simpler because no type information is associated with given-set names.

$$new\_givens : VARIETY \times \mathsf{F}\ NAME \to VARIETY$$

$$
\begin{aligned}
&new\_givens = \\
&\quad \lambda\ VARIETY_0;\ S : \mathsf{F}\ NAME\ | \\
&\qquad S \cap sig_0.given = \varnothing\ \bullet \\
&\quad \mu\ VARIETY\ | \\
&\qquad sig.given = sig_0.given \cup S\ \wedge \\
&\qquad sig.vars = sig_0.vars\ \wedge \\
&\qquad sig.type = sig_0.type\ \wedge \\
&\qquad models = \\
&\qquad\quad \{\ M : Struct(sig)\ |\ restrict\ sig_0\ M \in models_0\ \}.
\end{aligned}
$$

This completes the presentation of the denotational semantics of our Z-like specification language.

CHAPTER FOUR

DISCUSSION

This chapter contains discussions of various points which are raised by the semantic description of chapter 3, but for which space could not be found there. Section 4.1 discusses the important but semantically difficult notation for making generic definitions in Z specifications. Section 4.2 discusses the extent to which the semantics respects the principle of referential transparency. Section 4.3 examines a number of possible ways of handling partially defined terms in logic.

4.1 Generic definitions

Z provides notation for making definitions which have generic set parameters. An example is the definition of the inverse of a relation:

$$
\begin{array}{|l}
\underline{[X, Y]} \\
inv : (X \leftrightarrow Y) \to (Y \leftrightarrow X) \\
\hline
\forall R : X \leftrightarrow Y \bullet \\
\quad inv(R) = \{\, x : X;\ y : Y \mid x\,R\,y \bullet y \mapsto x \,\}
\end{array}
$$

Given this definition, we can write e.g. $inv[\mathsf{N}, CH]$ for a function which inverts relations in $\mathsf{N} \leftrightarrow CH$, and $inv[\mathsf{N}, \mathsf{N}]$ for one which inverts relations in $\mathsf{N} \leftrightarrow \mathsf{N}$, so that if $succ$ is the successor function on N and $pred$ the predecessor function, then

$$inv[\mathsf{N}, \mathsf{N}](succ) = pred.$$

Generic definitions like this are important, because they allow a versatile library of mathematical definitions to be built up independently of the particular sets to which they are applied. The definition above gives an inverse operation for each relation type, and allows an important mathematical idea to be captured abstractly. Without the facility for generic definitions, it would be necessary to introduce a separate definition of *inv* for each different relation type, and this would be clumsy.

In presenting a specification informally, the tendency is to omit the actual generic parameters, leaving them to be understood from the context, so that the equation above would be written

$inv(succ) = pred.$

It may be possible in a specification processing system to automate the insertion of the generic parameters: in this example, we know that *succ* and *pred* both have type $\mathbf{P}(\mathsf{N} \times \mathsf{N})$, so the occurrence of *inv* must have type

$\mathbf{P}(\mathbf{P}(\mathsf{N} \times \mathsf{N}) \times \mathbf{P}(\mathsf{N} \times \mathsf{N})).$

But $inv[X, Y]$ has type

$\mathbf{P}(\mathbf{P}(X \times Y) \times \mathbf{P}(Y \times X)),$

so we choose both parameters to be N. Note that $inv[\mathsf{N}, \mathsf{N} \setminus \{0\}]$ would also do, but a sensible default is to take the type itself as parameter. In most cases, the possibility of different parameters has no effect on the meaning, and where it does, the parameters can be inserted explicitly. Specification-processing tools can deduce the proper parameters using an algorithm similar to that described in (Milner, 1978).

The concepts of relation and partial function can themselves be captured using the notation of generic definitions:

$$
\begin{array}{l}
\underline{[X, Y]} \\
\quad REL, PFUN : \mathbf{P}(\mathbf{P}(X \times Y)) \\
\hline
\quad REL = \mathbf{P}(X \times Y) \\
\quad PFUN = \\
\qquad \{ f : REL \mid (\forall x : X; \, y, y' : Y \bullet x \, f \, y \wedge x \, f \, y' \Rightarrow y = y') \}
\end{array}
$$

Given this definition, we can regard the notations $X \leftrightarrow Y$ and $X \nrightarrow Y$ as abbreviations for $REL[X, Y]$ and $PFUN[X, Y]$ respectively, so even these notations can be made part of the standard library, and do not need to be built in to the language. The definition might be written more briefly as

$REL[X, Y] \;\widehat{=}\; \mathbf{P}(X \times Y)$

$PFUN[X, Y] \; \hat{=}$
$\qquad \{\, f : REL[X, Y] \mid (\forall\, x : X;\; y, y' : Y \bullet x f y \wedge x f y' \Rightarrow y = y')\,\},$

and this form of definition might be regarded as an abbreviation for the form above, the types of *REL* and *PFUN* being taken from the types of the defining expressions.

4.1.1 *A problem with the semantics*

In most of the examples met in practice, the meaning of a generic definition is clear: it introduces a family of constants, one for each possible collection of generic parameters. Because the axioms given in the body of the definition fix the values of these constants exactly, there is no possible ambiguity. But what happens if the axioms do not fix the values exactly, or even fail sometimes to be satisfiable at all? Suppose, for example, that the following definition were allowed:

$$
\begin{array}{|l}
\hline
\!=\![X]\!=\!=\!=\!=\!=\!=\!=\!=\!=\!=\!=\!=\!=\!=\!=\! \\
\; foo : X \\
\hline
\end{array}
$$

This just says that $foo[X]$ is a member of X, but doesn't give any information about which member of X is to be taken. Now suppose *foo* is used in a schema:

$$
\begin{array}{|l}
\hline
\; B \\
\hline
\; p : \mathbb{N} \\
\hline
\; p = foo[\mathbb{N}] \\
\hline
\end{array}
$$

Assume that a model for the global part of the specification is fixed. How many models are there of *B* which extend this model? If there is just one, then the choice of a model for the global part of the specification must fix the value of $foo[\mathbb{N}]$, and, in fact, the value of $foo[X]$ for each possible parameter value X. There are two problems with this: first, there is no acceptable value for the term $foo[\varnothing[\mathbb{N}]]$, in which the parameter is taken to be the empty set of natural numbers; second, since fixing $foo[X]$ for every X would involve making a choice from each of an infinite number of sets, existence of a global model could only be shown using the axiom of choice, and this seems rather counter-intuitive.

Suppose on the other hand that *B* has many models, each with a different value of *p*, so that fixing the global model does not fix the value of $foo[\mathbb{N}]$. In this case, the decorated schema B' will also have many models, and the conjunction $B \wedge B'$ will have models in which p and p' take different values. This is also counter-intuitive, because it ought to be possible to deduce $p = p'$ from the schema axioms $p = foo[\mathbb{N}]$ and $p' = foo[\mathbb{N}]$, together with symmetry and transitivity of equality.

A solution is to restrict generic global definitions so that there must be a unique model of the defining schema for each value of the generic parameters. This restriction is obeyed by all the definitions in the standard mathematical library.

4.1.2 *Semantics of generic definitions*

A semantics can be given to generic definitions, provided they define exactly the values of their constants for each possible assignment of values to the generic parameters.

The semantic domain *GMEANING* for generic definitions is the same as that for schemas: we simply record the meaning of the schema given as the definition.

$$GMEANING \;\cong\; SMEANING$$

To fit in with the global part of an environment ρ, a generic definition must be in the set $Gmeaning(\rho.global)$ of definitions which satisfy the uniqueness condition referred to above.

$$
\begin{array}{|l}
Gmeaning : VARIETY \rightarrow \mathbf{P}\ GMEANING \\
\hline
Gmeaning(V_0) = \\
\quad \{\ GMEANING \mid \\
\qquad basis(local.sig)\ \text{subsig}\ V_0.sig\ \wedge \\
\qquad (\forall\, M : V_0.models;\ aparam : seq[W] \mid \\
\qquad\quad \#aparam = \#fparam \bullet \\
\qquad \exists!\, M' : local.models \bullet \\
\qquad\quad restrict\,(basis(local.sig))\ M \\
\qquad\qquad = restrict\,(basis(local.sig))\ M' \wedge \\
\qquad M'.val \circ (tag\ 1) \circ fparam = aparam)\ \}.
\end{array}
$$

The uniqueness condition says that if we choose a model M for the global part of the specification and choose the values of the formal generic parameters, then the definition should have a unique model consistent with these choices, that is, a unique model M' which agrees with M on their common signature and gives the specified values to the formal parameters.

The notion of environment must be extended to allow generic definitions to be recorded: we add a new component *gdict*, mapping the identifiers of

generic constants to the content of their definitions. The new component is
subject to two axioms: first, that the definitions must fit in with the global
part of the environment sensibly, and second, that they should actually
define the constants they claim to define.

> *ENV* _____
> $\dots$
>
> *gdict* : *IDENT* $\nrightarrow$ *GMEANING*
>
> $\dots$
>
> $\forall x$: dom *gdict* $\bullet$
>   *gdict* $x \in$ *Gmeaning(global)* $\wedge$
> $x \in$ *locids((gdict x).local.sig.vars)*

Of course, all the operations which manipulate environments without
reference to generic definitions must be redefined so that they copy the *gdict*
component unaltered. There is a slight problem with the *enrich* operation,
in that we must check that enriching the global part of the specification does
not destroy the uniqueness condition on any generic definitions which may
be present, but this is a trivial consequence of the fact that 'restricting in
two steps is the same as restricting in one' (compare subsection 2.3.2).

Now the syntax of specifications can be extended to allow generic definitions:

$$SPEC ::= \dots \mid \mathbf{define}\ [IDENT, \dots, IDENT]\ SCHEMA\ \mathbf{end}$$

The meaning of a generic definition is rather like that of a schema definition,
except that the new variety is added as a series of entries in *gdict*, one for
each of the constants defined.

> *spec* : *ENV* $\rightarrow$ *SPEC* $\nrightarrow$ *ENV*
>
> $\dots$
>
> *spec* $\rho\, k$ $[\mathbf{define}\ [x_1, \dots, x_n]\ s\ \mathbf{end}] \cong$
> $\mu\, \rho_1 : ENV \mid \rho_1 \cong$
>   *enrich*$(\rho,\ new\_givens(\rho.global,\ tag\ 1\ [\{x_1, \dots, x_n\}]))\ \bullet$
> $\mu\, gm : GMEANING \mid$
>   *gm.local* $\cong$ *schema* $\rho_1\ 1\ [s]\ \wedge$
>   *gm.fparam* $= \langle x_1, \dots, x_n \rangle\ \bullet$
>   *add_defs*(ρ, gm).

The auxiliary function *add_defs* adds the new definitions to *gdict*, provided they satisfy the proper conditions, and no attempt is being made to give more one definition to the same identifier.

$add\_defs : ENV \times GMEANING \rightarrow\!\!\!\rightarrow ENV$

$$add\_defs =$$
$$\lambda\,\rho : ENV;\, gm : GMEANING\,|$$
$$\quad gm \in Gmeaning(\rho.global) \wedge$$
$$\quad locids(gm.local.sig.vars) \cap \mathrm{dom}\,\rho.gdict = \varnothing \,\bullet$$
$$\mu\,\rho' : ENV\,|$$
$$\quad \rho'.global = \rho.global \wedge$$
$$\quad \rho'.sdict = \rho.sdict \wedge$$
$$\quad \rho'.gdict =$$
$$\quad\quad \rho.gdict \cup \{\,x : locids(gm.local.sig.vars) \bullet x \mapsto gm\,\}$$

So much for defining generic constants: how can they be used? We introduce a new kind of term, an applied occurrence of a generic constant:

$$TERM ::= \ldots \mid IDENT[TERM, \ldots, TERM]$$

The well-typing rule assigns to such a term the type found by instantiating the definition and taking the type of the identifier in this:

$$V \cong instantiate(\rho.global, k, \rho.gdict(x), blank,$$
$$\qquad\qquad\qquad map\,(term\,\rho\,k)\,\langle t_1, \ldots, t_n\rangle)$$
$$V.sig.type(tag\,k\,x) = a$$
$$\overline{\rule{0pt}{1.2em}\rho, k \vdash x[t_1, \ldots, t_n] :: a}$$

The value of the term in a model M is the value of x in the unique model M' of V which agrees with M:

$$V \cong instantiate(\rho.global, k, \rho.gdict(x), blank,$$
$$\qquad\qquad\qquad map\,(term\,\rho\,k)\,\langle t_1, \ldots, t_n\rangle)$$
$$M' \in V.models$$
$$restrict\,\rho.global.sig\,M' = M$$
$$\overline{\rule{0pt}{1.2em}\rho, k, M \vdash x[t_1, \ldots, t_n] \Rightarrow \dot{M}'.val(tag\,k\,x)}$$

This evaluation rule gives a unique value to the term in each model M. For a proof of this, let V_1 be the variety constructed in the definition of *instantiate* which combines $\rho.global$ with the retagged local variables and formal parameters. The models of the result of *instantiate* are those obtained by fixing the values of the formal parameters in models of V_1. An antecedent of the rule is that

$restrict\ \rho.global.sig\ M' = M,$

so, in particular,

$restrict\ basis(gm.local.sig)\ M' = restrict\ basis(gm.local.sig)\ M,$

where $gm = \rho.gdict(x)$, since $basis(gm.local.sig)$ subsig $\rho.global.sig$. This means, because of the uniqueness condition, that fixing the formal parameters gives a unique model, and this property is not affected by the renaming of local variables and formal parameters. The value of the term is just the value of x in this unique model.

4.2 Referential transparency

There are two places on the semantics where referential transparency seems to be compromised, and it is perhaps worth discussing them here. A definition of the term 'referential transparency' is given in (Stoy, 1977):

> We use it to refer to the fact of mathematics which says: "The only thing which matters about an expression is its value, and any subexpression can be replaced by any other equal in value. Moreover, the value of an expression is, within certain limits, the same wherever it occurs."

One place where this principle seems to be violated is in the notion of the 'characteristic tuple' of a schema body. For example, if FOO is the schema

```
┌─FOO ────────────────
│  x, y : N
│──────────────────────
│  x > y
└──────────────────────
```

then the term $\{ FOO \}$ is equivalent to

$\{ FOO \bullet \theta FOO \}$

and thus has type $\mathbf{P}\{x, y : \mathbb{N}\}$—it is a set of bindings. But if we replace the applied occurrence of FOO with its defining text—which has, in this context, the same value as a variety—the resulting term

$\{ x, y : \mathbb{N} \mid x > y \}$

is equivalent to

$$\{\, x, y : \mathsf{N} \mid x > y \bullet (x, y) \,\}$$

and so has type $\mathsf{P}(\mathsf{N} \times \mathsf{N})$—it is a set of pairs of numbers. In effect, the function *char_tuple* is a second semantic function for schema bodies, and this existence of two independent semantic functions is a symptom of violation of referential transparency.

Another violation is connected with θ-terms. Taking FOO to be the schema defined above, and defining BAZ by

$$BAZ \;\hat{=}\; FOO',$$

we find that $\theta FOO'$ has type $\langle x, y : \mathsf{N} \rangle$ according to the well-typing rule for θ-terms, but θBAZ has type $\langle x', y' : \mathsf{N} \rangle$. This apparent anomaly can be explained by noting that the term $\theta FOO'$ does not in fact contain FOO' as a sub-expression: in fact the only sub-expressions are FOO and $'$ themselves.

Both these examples of referential opacity could be removed with appropriate changes to the semantics: we could, for example, make the term

$$\{\, x, y : \mathsf{N} \mid x > y \,\}$$

have type $\mathsf{P}\langle x, y : \mathsf{N} \rangle$, and make $\theta FOO'$ have type $\langle x', y' : \mathsf{N} \rangle$, with appropriate changes to the value rules as well, but the existing semantics turns out to be more useful in practice. The first notation is useful for defining relations by comprehension, and the second is useful in predicates such as

$$\theta FOO' = \theta FOO,$$

which typically asserts that the state FOO does not change in an operation.

4.3   Partially defined terms

The semantics of predicates in section 3.5 fixed the behaviour of undefined terms under equality with the equation

$$pred\ \rho\,k\ [\![t_1 = t_2]\!] \;\hat{=}$$
$$\mu\ tt_1, tt_2 : TMEANING \mid$$
$$\qquad tt_1 \;\hat{=}\; term\ \rho\,k\ [\![t_1]\!]$$
$$\qquad tt_2 \;\hat{=}\; term\ \rho\,k\ [\![t_2]\!]$$
$$\qquad tt_1.type = tt_2.type.$$
$$\{\, M : \rho.global.models \mid$$
$$\qquad M \in (\mathrm{dom}\ tt_1.eval) \cap (\mathrm{dom}\ tt_2.eval) \wedge$$
$$\qquad tt_1.eval(M) = tt_2.eval(M) \,\}.$$

This says that '$t_1 = t_2$' is true (assuming t_1 and t_2 have the same type) exactly when both t_1 and t_2 are defined and their values are equal, and false otherwise. A similar equation said that '$t_1 \in t_2$' is true (assuming t_1 has type a and t_2 has type $\mathbf{P}\ a$ for some type a) exactly when both t_1 and t_2 are defined and the value of t_1 is an element of whatever set is the value of t_2.

These definitions lead to a perfectly consistent logic of partially defined terms, but they might be criticized for failing to capture faithfully our intuitive understanding of the equality and membership predicates: if one of t_1 and t_2 is undefined, then we think of '$t_1 = t_2$' as making no sense, rather than as being false in the usual way. In particular, we are reluctant to accept that '$\neg\ t_1 = t_2$' is true in this case.

These considerations have led some authors to reject classical logic, in which there are two truth-values *true* and *false*, in favour of a 'three-valued' system with an extra truth-value *undefined*, or more precisely, the possibility that a sentence will have a 'gap' in its truth-values. Barringer, Cheng, and Jones (1984), in a paper intended for computer scientists, propose such a system, and similar systems are studied in the D.Phil. thesis of Blamey (1980).

In these systems, the equation '$t_1 = t_2$' will have truth-value *undefined* unless both t_1 and t_2 are defined, and if so, it takes value *true* just if their values are equal. The classical connectives are replaced by three-valued connectives which agree with them on *true* and *false*, and are monotonic with respect to a partial ordering on truth-values which makes *true* and *false* greater than *undefined*. For example, the truth-tables for negation, conjunction and implication are as follows:

$\neg$			$\wedge$	t	f	u		$\Rightarrow$	t	f	u
t	f		t	t	f	u		t	t	f	u
f	t		f	f	f	f		f	t	t	t
u	u		u	u	f	u		u	t	u	u

These are the connectives which are defined whenever possible whilst still being monotonic.

An unfortunate feature of this logic is that classical tautologies are not preserved: for example, the sentence $P \Rightarrow P$ is not tautological, for it takes value *undefined* when P is itself *undefined*. What is more, the deduction theorem fails for the logic, for given that Q can be deduced from P, we are not entitled to conclude that $P \Rightarrow Q$ unless we can show separately that P is not *undefined*.

However, the three-valued logic fits in well with the VDM style of specification (Jones, 1980), where properties of objects are represented by Boolean-valued functions. In this style, the property of being an even number would be represented as follows:

$$is\text{-}even : Nat0 \to Bool$$
$$is\text{-}even(x) \;\hat{=}\; (x \bmod 2) = 0$$

The use of Boolean-valued terms such as *is-even*(3) as predicates already introduces the possibility that predicates will be undefined, and this makes it quite natural to explain the notation in terms of a logic with truth-value gaps. The equality predicate can be regarded as a Boolean-valued function which is strict: if, in the equation '$t_1 = t_2$', one or both of the terms t_1 and t_2 are undefined, then the whole equation simply has undefined truth-value.

By way of contrast, the Z style is to represent a property by the set of objects which possess the property, so that the same idea would be expressed as:

$$even : \mathbb{P}\,\mathbb{N}$$
$$even = \{\, x : \mathbb{N} \mid (x \bmod 2) = 0 \,\}$$

This seems to fit in better with two-valued logic, for we think of sets as definitely including or excluding each of their potential elements, with no room for a third possibility.

Abrial, in his formulation of logic and set theory for program specification and development—see, for example, (Abrial, 1984b)—treats partial functions by giving an axiom which allows us to reason about the values of functions applied inside their domain, but allows little or nothing to be deduced about what happens outside the domain: one formulation is

$$f \in S_1 \nrightarrow S_2 \wedge (\exists y : S_2 \bullet (t, y) \in f) \Rightarrow (t, f(t)) \in f.$$

Here the idea is that $f(t)$ should be a term which always has some value, but no information is given about this value unless f is a function and t is in its domain. One possible interpretation is that $f(t)$ always has the same arbitrarily-chosen value—the empty set, say—whenever t is outside the domain of f, but other interpretations may make $f(t)$ behave in an utterly wild way under these circumstances, and this is not ruled out by the axiom.

The result of this is a two-valued logic in which, of course, '$t_1 = t_2$' always has some truth-value, but the axiom for function-application will not

always allow us to tell which—it is incomplete. The propositional connectives and the quantifiers retain their classical interpretation, however, and
all the classical tautologies continue to be valid.

The logic of partial functions given by Abrial's approach can be reflected
in the model-based semantics by giving an intentionally incomplete definition of the semantics of predicates. The semantic equation at the beginning
of this section might be replaced by the following:

$$pred\ \rho\,k\ [\![t_1 = t_2]\!] \cong$$
$$\mu\ tt_1, tt_2 : TMEANING\ |$$
$$tt_1 \cong term\ \rho\,k\ [\![t_1]\!]$$
$$tt_2 \cong term\ \rho\,k\ [\![t_2]\!]$$
$$tt_1.type = tt_2.type.$$
$$equality(tt_1.eval, tt_2.eval) \cap \rho.global.models$$

with the function *equality* being specified by

$$equality : (STRUCT \nrightarrow W) \times (STRUCT \nrightarrow W) \to \mathbb{P}\ STRUCT$$

$$\forall M : \operatorname{dom} f \cap \operatorname{dom} g \bullet$$
$$M \in equality(f, g) \Leftrightarrow f(M) = g(M)$$

This function is specified incompletely: the axiom says only what happens
to structures in the domain of both its arguments. We regard as valid those
predicates—or, in a sequent calculus, those sequents—which are true in
every model of a specification and under any possible choice of the *equality*
function. Sound inference rules in such a calculus are those which preserve
validity.

The reason for defining soundness as preservation of validity rather than
preservation of truth is that validity behaves well under extension of the
environment, and this is important in a calculus of schemas such as the one
described in chapter 5.

4.4   Z and Clear

As we saw in chapter 1, Clear specifications consist of a collection of theories,
and like schemas, theories have an alphabet of components: in Clear these
are called the operations of the theory. Although the style in which theories
are used is quite different from the Z style of using schemas, both languages
have facilities for combining these structural units, and both make some
provision for parametrized specification units.

4.4.1 *Theories and varieties*

In their semantics for Clear, Burstall and Goguen (1980) begin by introducing signatures: each signature contains a set of sort names and a set of operation names associated with sorts for the arguments and result. They then define, for each signature Σ, both a set $Eqn(\Sigma)$ of equations and a set $Alg(\Sigma)$ of algebras. For ordinary Clear, the equations are universally-quantified equations between terms, although it is possible to allow more general forms such as conditional equations. The algebras are *heterogeneous algebras* (Burstall & Goguen, 1982); they assign a carrier set to each sort and a total function to each operation. The domain of an operation is the Cartesian product of the carriers of its argument sorts, and its range is contained in the carrier of its result sort.

For each signature Σ there is a relation

$$\models_{\Sigma}: Alg(\Sigma) \leftrightarrow Eqn(\Sigma)$$

of *satisfaction* between models and sentences for the same signature Σ. An algebra satisfies an equation if, whatever value the variables take, both sides of the equation take the same value in the algebra. If S is a set of equations over Σ, S^* is the set of algebras which satisfy each equation in S:

$$S^* = \{\, m : Mod(\Sigma) \mid (\forall\, e \in S \bullet m \models_{\Sigma} e)\,\};$$

If we think of S as specifying an algebra which satisfies all the equations, then S^* is the set of algebras which satisfy the specification. Similarly, if V is a set of models for Σ, then $V^{\dagger}$ is the set of all sentences satisfied by each model in V:

$$V^{\dagger} = \{\, e \in Sen(\Sigma) \mid (\forall\, m \in V \bullet m \models_{\Sigma} e)\,\}.$$

Together, the maps $S \mapsto S^*$ and $V \mapsto V^{\dagger}$ give a Galois connection (Birkhoff, 1967) between sets of sentences and sets of models. If $S_1 \subseteq S_2$ then $S_2^* \subseteq S_1^*$: strengthening the specification can only decrease the set of algebras which satisfy it. Conversely, if $V_1 \subseteq V_2$ then $V_2^{\dagger} \subseteq V_1^{\dagger}$. Also $S \subseteq S^{*\dagger}$ and $V \subseteq V^{\dagger *}$. This means that there is a closure operation $S \mapsto S^{\circ}$ on sets of sentences given by $S^{\circ} = S^{*\dagger}$. This is the operation of *closure under semantic entailment*: the sentences in S° are all those which hold in every model satisfying all the axioms in S.

A *theory* is a pair (Σ, S) where Σ is a signature and S is a closed set of sentences over Σ, and theories are taken as the fundamental concept in the semantics of Clear. If S is a set of axioms over Σ forming a specification, the meaning of the specification, to put it simply, is taken as the theory

(Σ, S°) obtained by taking the closure of S. The closure operation provides abstraction from the details of how the equations are formulated: two specifications with different but logically equivalent equations will give the same theory. Clear also provides more expressive means of denoting theories than a simple presentation of signature and axioms; theories may be described by combining and enriching other theories, and the **data** operation allows theories closed under mathematical induction.

Variety-based semantics can be explained in the same framework: there is a closure operation $V \mapsto V^{\bullet}$ on sets of models analogous to $S \mapsto S^{\circ}$, given by $V^{\bullet} = V^{\dagger *}$, and a variety is a pair (Σ, V) where V is a closed set of models over Σ. The meaning of a specification with axioms S is the variety (Σ, S^{*}). Because of the Galois connection, S^{*} is a closed set of models, and there is a bijective correspondence between closed sets of sentences and closed sets of models given by $S \mapsto S^{*}$; its inverse is $V \mapsto V^{\dagger}$. This means that theory-based and variety-based semantics are in a sense equivalent, at least in the logical framework underlying Clear.

This pleasing symmetry is not easy to generalize to Z, however. The predicates in Z specifications are rather more complicated than the simple equations of Clear. They may mention schema-names, so an environment of schema-definitions as well as a signature is needed to make sense of a predicate, and a set of predicates closed under entailment in one environment will not remain closed when further schemas are added: there will be extra predicates mentioning the new schema-names, and some of these will be entailed by the predicates of the theory. This instability under change of environment makes theories less attractive as a semantic concept, but it is a disadvantage from which varieties do not suffer.

Another advantage of variety-based semantics for Z is that the operation of comprehension can easily be described as an operation on the class of models of a schema, and this seems more natural than describing it as an operation on predicates. Variety-based semantics has its uses in algebraic specification too: Sannella and Wirsing use it for their specification language ASL (1983) because ASL's notion of behavioural abstraction is best described in terms of models.

4.4.2 *The categorical view*
In the semantics for Clear mentioned above, the semantic spaces are constructed using concepts from category theory. A *category* (Mac Lane, 1971) consists of a class of 'objects' with some 'arrows', each linking one object to another. There is an operation of composition which can combine an arrow

from A to B with another from B to C, resulting in an arrow from A to C. Composition must be associative, and there are 'identity arrows' for all the objects which act as left and right identities for composition. Examples of categories occur in many branches of mathematics: the simplest example is the category **Set** of sets, in which the objects are sets and the arrows total functions from one set to another. A few other examples are

- Sets and partial functions or relations,

- Groups and group homomorphisms,

- Topological spaces and continuous functions,

- Scott domains and approximable maps.

A *functor* is a mapping of the objects and arrows of one category on the objects and arrows of another; this mapping must respect the composition and the identity arrows. The collection of all (sufficiently small) categories and functors between them itself forms a category **Cat**.

The semantics of Clear uses categories at two levels. The structures described by Clear specifications are heterogeneous algebras, and these form a category in which the arrows are homomorphisms, mappings from the carriers of one algebra to the carriers of another which preserve the operations. The **data** operation of Clear specifies algebras which contain 'no junk'—the algebra contains no elements that cannot be reached using the operations—and suffer from 'no confusion'—the only equations which hold are those which follow from the axioms. These algebras can be characterized elegantly in categorical terms: they are 'initial objects' in the category of algebras which satisfy the axioms.

At another level, Burstall and Goguen introduce not only a notion of signature, but also morphisms between signatures. These morphisms map the names of one signature into the names of another in a way that preserves the types, and signatures with signature morphisms constitute a category **Sig**. Signature morphisms are made to act on sentences and models by renaming, and this gives rise to functors **Eqn** : **Sig** $\rightarrow$ **Set** and **Alg** : **Sig**^{op} $\rightarrow$ **Cat**; the actions of these functors on objects are the functions *Alg* and *Eqn* mentioned in subsection 4.4.1.

From these functors and the satisfaction relation $\models$, a very general construction gives a category of theories, in which the objects are theories as described above, and the arrows are special signature morphisms which preserve the truth of equations. Clear texts have theories as their meaning, and

theory morphisms are used to show how the parts of a modular specification
fit together. Once it has been shown that theories can be put together in
a very few simple ways, general results from category theory ensure that
more complex constructions will be possible, for example those involved in
the application of a theory procedure to actual theory parameters.

The great attraction of this approach is that the semantics of the specification language can be made largely independent of the logic which is used
to write the axioms in a specification. This means that the same operations
for structuring specifications can be used with different specification for-
malisms. In a later paper (Goguen & Burstall, 1984), the authors introduce
the notion of an *institution*, an abstract logical framework, and show how
the Clear semantics can be made to work for a large class of institutions.
Many different logics can be viewed as institutions, and hence used to write
Clear specifications. The authors also introduce the notion of an *institution
morphism*. Together with institutions, these form a category, and by relating two logical frameworks with an institution morphism, it is possible to
write specifications partly in one logic and partly in another. The use of the
concept of institution to abstract from details of the logic is also discussed
in (Sannella & Tarlecki, 1984).

Categorical notions also underlie the semantics for Z given in chapter 3,
but because the specification-structuring operations in Z—the operations
of the schema-calculus—rely on identification of variables with the same
name, most of the signature morphisms are implicit in the *inclusion* of
one signature in another. The function *restrict* shows how inclusions of
signatures can be made to act on structures, and this is closely analogous
to the situation in Clear. The property of *restrict* that restricting in two
steps is the same as restricting in one step is analogous to the fact that the
action of signature morphisms is a functor, and the relation subvar between
varieties plays for us the part of the theory morphisms in Clear.

CHAPTER FIVE

STUDIES IN Z STYLE

This chapter examines several aspects of the use of Z from the point of view of the formal semantics. We look first at ways of reasoning about modular specifications which allow the structure of the proof to mimic the structure of the specification. The next section shows how even the most basic types—for example the natural numbers—can be specified in Z, and incidentally demonstrates how Z specifications can be developed in a way which makes their consistency provable. Section 5.3 explores the relationship between Z specifications, which at the most abstract level just describe certain sets, and abstract data types, conceived as having a state-space and operations with input and output. The final section discusses the need for non-determinism in specifications, even when programs are deterministic.

5.1 Reasoning about specifications

Specifications of large systems in Z are often built up by specifying smaller sub-systems using schemas, then combining these schemas with the operations of the schema calculus. One common technique is to describe first the operation of a system under the assumption that its input is correct, and to add later a description of the action to be taken in case of incorrect input. This modular style makes the specification easier to understand, although it does not necessarily reflect the form of an implementation, in which it may be necessary to mingle code for dealing with errors in the input with code for dealing with normal operation.

Proofs of results about modular specifications will be easier to understand if they follow the structure of the specification, so that the reader's attention can be focussed first on one part of the specification and then on another. For example, to show that an operation satisfies some invariance property when its effects for correct and for incorrect input are specified separately, it would be desirable to prove the invariance for each case on its own, then combine these results to deduce that the invariance property holds for the operation as a whole. This style of proof needs inference rules which allow results about fragments of a specification to be drawn together to derive a result about the whole specification.

5.1.1 *An example*
Suppose we are specifying a simple banking system. We begin by deciding that the state of the system consists of the balance of each account:

$$
\begin{array}{|l}
\hline
\text{\_\_}BANK \text{\_\_} \\
\hline
bal : ACCT \rightarrow \mathbb{N} \\
\hline
\end{array}
$$

$$\Delta BANK \,\;\hat{=}\; BANK \wedge BANK'$$

$$\Xi BANK \,\;\hat{=}\; [\,\Delta BANK \mid bal' = bal\,]$$

The balances are (say) numbers of pence, and we suppose that the bank manager is mean enough never to allow overdrafts.

One possible operation is to transfer some money from one account to another:

$$
\begin{array}{|l}
\hline
\text{\_\_}Transfer1 \text{\_\_} \\
\Delta BANK \\
amount? : \mathbb{N} \\
src?, dst? : ACCT \\
\hline
src? \neq dst? \\
bal(src?) \geq amount? \\
bal' = bal \oplus \{src? \mapsto bal(src?) - amount?, \\
\qquad\qquad\qquad\quad dst? \mapsto bal(dst?) + amount?\} \\
\hline
\end{array}
$$

The transfer can take place only if the source and destination accounts are different and the source account contains enough money. If so, the balance of the source account is reduced by the amount to be transferred, and the balance of the destination account is increased by the same amount.

We might describe also the operations of depositing and withdrawing money from the bank, asking for the current balance of an account, and so on, then turn later to the reporting of invalid operations. To do this, we add an extra output *report!* to each operation, and arrange that this has value 'OK' after every successful operation:

```
┌─ Ok ──────────────────────────────────
│ report! : MESSAGE
├───────────────────────────────────────
│ report! = 'OK'
└───────────────────────────────────────
```

For unsuccessful operations, we report the reason for failure with an appropriate message, and constrain the final state of the banking system to be the same as the initial state. The two possible errors in a *Transfer* operation occur when the source and destination accounts are the same, and when the source account does not contain enough money:

```
┌─ SameAcct ────────────────────────────
│ ΞBANK
│ src?, dst? : ACCT
│ report! : MESSAGE
├───────────────────────────────────────
│ src? = dst?
│ report! = 'Same account for src and dst'
└───────────────────────────────────────
```

```
┌─ NotEnough ───────────────────────────
│ ΞBANK
│ amount? : N
│ src? : ACCT
│ report! : MESSAGE
├───────────────────────────────────────
│ bal(src?) < amount
│ report! = 'Not enough money in src'
└───────────────────────────────────────
```

The transfer operation, complete with error reporting, can now be specified by combining these schemas:

$$Transfer \; \hat{=} \; (Transfer1 \land Ok) \lor SameAcct \lor NotEnough.$$

Error reporting for other operations might be specified in the same concise way:

$$Withdraw \; \hat{=} \; (Withdraw1 \land Ok) \lor NotEnough.$$

Having specified the operations in this nicely modular way, we might want to prove that they have certain properties, either to check that the specification captures our customer's requirements or to prove the correctness of a proposed refinement. As an example, suppose we want to check that in a *Transfer* operation, no matter what the input parameters, the total amount of money in the source and destination accounts remains unchanged:

$$bal'(src?) + bal'(dst?) = bal(src?) + bal(dst?).$$

How might we prove this? A *Transfer* operation consists of either a successful *Transfer*1 operation, or one of the two error operations *SameAcct* or *NotEnough*. In the first case we have

$$bal'(src?) = bal(src?) - amount?$$
$$bal'(dst?) = bal(dst?) + amount?,$$

and adding these together gives the desired result. In the case of the error operations, we have from $\Xi BANK$ the equation

$$bal' = bal,$$

from which the desired result follows immediately.

So the result is quite easy to prove for each of the disjuncts in the *Transfer* operation; to combine these into a result about the *Transfer* operation itself, what is needed is a formal means for reasoning about the operations of the schema calculus.

5.1.2 *A calculus of schemas*

Reasoning from the axioms of each of the schemas combined in the *Transfer* operation has enabled us to show that, in each case, the total balance of source and destination accounts is preserved. Formally, we might record this by means of *sequents* such as

$$Transfer1 \vdash bal'(src?) + bal'(dst?) = bal(src?) + bal(dst?).$$

To derive our desired result, namely

$$Transfer \vdash bal'(src?) + bal'(dst?) = bal(src?) + bal(dst?),$$

we need inference rules which allow schema operations to be introduced into the expression on the left of the $\vdash$. One such rule is

$$\frac{A \vdash p}{A \wedge B \vdash p.}$$

If p is a consequence of a schema A, then it is reasonable to suppose that it is a consequence of $A \wedge B$ also. This is true in the simplest language of schemas, but when the environment includes global variables, it is subject to the condition that no free variables of p become captured by the declarations in B. Writing $fv(p)$ for the set of free variables of p, and

$$v(B) = locids((\rho.sdict\ B).local.sig.vars)$$

for the variables of B, the condition becomes

$$fv(p) \cap v(B) \subseteq v(A).$$

Of course, there is a mirror-image rule:

$$\frac{B \vdash p}{A \wedge B \vdash p.} \quad [\,fv(p) \cap v(A) \subseteq v(B)\,]$$

For disjunction, the rule requires that p be established for each of the arguments separately:

$$\frac{\begin{array}{c} A \vdash p \\ B \vdash p \end{array}}{A \vee B \vdash p.} \quad [\,fv(p) \cap (v(A) \cup v(B)) \subseteq v(A) \cap v(B)\,]$$

The free-variable condition says that all free variables of p bound by either A or B must be bound by both of them. The schema projection operator $\upharpoonright$ has a simple rule:

$$\frac{A \vdash p}{A \upharpoonright B \vdash p.} \quad [\,fv(p) \cap v(A) \subseteq v(B)\,]$$

This says that any consequence of A is also a consequence of $A \upharpoonright B$, provided it contains no variables of A which are not also variables of B. The strong definition of projection (compare section 2.5) also obeys the rule

$$\frac{B \vdash p}{A \upharpoonright B \vdash p.}$$

Using these rules, we can prove our desired result about the *Transfer* operation. The results already proved are

(1) $Transfer1 \vdash bal'(src?) + bal'(dst?) = bal(src?) + bal(dst?)$,

(2) $SameAcct \vdash bal'(src?) + bal'(dst?) = bal(src?) + bal(dst?)$,

(3) *NotEnough* $\vdash$ $bal'(src?) + bal'(dst?) = bal(src?) + bal(dst?)$.

Now the first rule for introducing $\wedge$ allows us to derive from (1)

(4) *Transfer1* $\wedge$ *OK* $\vdash$ $bal'(src?) + bal'(dst?) = bal(src?) + bal(dst?)$,

and two applications of the rule for introducing $\vee$ allow us to derive successively

(5) *(Transfer1* $\wedge$ *OK)* $\vee$ *SameAcct* $\vdash$
$\qquad bal'(src?) + bal'(dst?) = bal(src?) + bal(dst?)$ from (4) and (2),

(6) *(Transfer1* $\wedge$ *OK)* $\vee$ *SameAcct* $\vee$ *NotEnough* $\vdash$
$\qquad bal'(src?) + bal'(dst?) = bal(src?) + bal(dst?)$ from (5) and (3).

The next subsection defines formally the syntax and semantics of sequents, and shows how the soundness of the inference rules can be proved.

5.1.3 *Soundness of the rules*
The syntax of sequents is

$\qquad$ *SEQUENT* ::= *SEXP* $\vdash$ *PRED*.

Given an environment ρ obtained by evaluating a Z specification, we can say whether such a sequent is *valid* or *invalid*: the sequent

$\qquad se \vdash p$

is valid if and only if, in the environment ρ enriched with *se*, every model of the global variety satisfies *p*. Formally, if

$\qquad \rho_1 = enrich(\rho, sexp\, \rho\, 1\, [\![se]\!])$,

then the sequent is valid in ρ if and only if

$\qquad pred\, \rho_1\, 1\, [\![p]\!] = \rho_1.global.models$.

As usual, we say that an inference rule is *sound* if applying it to valid antecedents always gives a valid consequent. The proof of soundness for the first $\wedge$-rule,

$$\frac{A \vdash p}{A \wedge B \vdash p,} \qquad [\, fv(p) \cap v(B) \subseteq v(A)\,]$$

is along the following lines: let

$\qquad V_1 = sexp\, \rho\, 1\, [\![A]\!]$,   and $\rho_1 = enrich(\rho, V_1)$;
$\qquad V_2 = sexp\, \rho\, 1\, [\![A \wedge B]\!]$,   and $\rho_2 = enrich(\rho, V_2)$.

Suppose $M_2 \in V_2.models$, and let $M_1 = restrict\ V_1.sig\ M_2$. By the definition of schema conjunction, $M_1 \in V_1.models$. The first thing to show is that every term t which satisfies the side-condition,

$$fv(t) \cap v(B) \subseteq v(A), \qquad\qquad\qquad (*)$$

is defined in M_1 exactly if it is defined in M_2, and if so, it has the same value in both models. In the notation of section 3.4, we must show that

$$\rho_1, 1, M_1 \vdash t \Rightarrow u$$

if and only if

$$\rho_2, 1, M_2 \vdash t \Rightarrow u.$$

This is proved by structural induction on t. To deal with the quantifier-like constructs which introduce local variables, it is necessary to generalize the result slightly before appealing to induction. We need to show that the desired equivalence holds for all pairs of environments ρ_1' and ρ_2' obtained by enriching ρ_1 and ρ_2 with the same declarations, and all pairs of models M_1' and M_2' related by restriction in the same way as M_1 and M_2. (Strictly speaking, we ought also to check that t is well-typed in ρ_1 if and only if it is well-typed in ρ_2, and that the types are the same).

For identifiers x, the free-variable condition $(*)$ is exactly what is needed to ensure that x has the same referent in both ρ_1 and ρ_2, i.e. that

$$find\ (\rho_1.global.sig, 1)\ x = find\ (\rho_2.global.sig, 1)\ x,$$

and this, together with the fact that M_1 is a restriction of M_2, gives the required result. The proof for simple term-constructors such as tupling goes through quite simply: the evaluation rule for tuples means that

$$\rho_1, 1, M_1 \vdash (t_1, \ldots, t_n) \Rightarrow tuple\ \langle u_1, \ldots, u_n \rangle$$

if and only if

$$\rho_1, 1, M_1 \vdash t_i \Rightarrow u_i \quad (1 \leq i \leq n),$$

and, by the induction hypothesis, this is so if and only if

$$\rho_2, 1, M_2 \vdash t_i \Rightarrow u_i \quad (1 \leq i \leq n),$$

which is equivalent to

$$\rho_2, 1, M_2 \vdash (t_1, \ldots, t_n) \Rightarrow tuple\ \langle u_1, \ldots, u_n \rangle.$$

The same kind of argument applies to all those terms whose values are functions of the values of their sub-terms in the same environment.

For term-constructors such as set-comprehension which introduce a new scope, the extra generality of the induction hypothesis is needed: we need to compare the behaviour of models in the enriched environment of the new scope. Also, the mutual recursion between the syntax of predicates and terms means that, strictly speaking, a mutual induction is needed at this point.

Once it is established that terms behave the same in M_1 and M_2, attention can be turned to predicates. We aim to show that M_1 satisfies p if and only if M_2 does, i.e. that

$$M_1 \in pred\ \rho_1\ 1\ [\![p]\!]$$

if and only if

$$M_2 \in pred\ \rho_2\ 1\ [\![p]\!],$$

provided that p satisfies the free-variable condition of the inference rule. Again, the result must be generalized before applying induction to take into account the possibility of nested scopes, but the details are omitted here.

For the simplest predicates **true** and **false**, the result is immediate, and for equations '$t_1 = t_2$' and membership predicates '$t_1 \in t_2$', it follows from the result proved above for terms, for the truth-conditions of these predicates depend only on the definedness and values of t_1 and t_2, at least in the semantics of section 3.5.

For the propositional connectives, the definition of the semantic function *pred* together with the induction hypothesis is enough: for example, if

$$M_1 \in pred\ \rho_1\ 1\ [\![p_1 \lor p_2]\!]$$

then

$$M_1 \in pred\ \rho_1\ 1\ [\![p_1]\!] \quad \text{or} \quad M_1 \in pred\ \rho_1\ 1\ [\![p_2]\!],$$

so, by the induction hypothesis,

$$M_2 \in pred\ \rho_2\ 1\ [\![p_1]\!] \quad \text{or} \quad M_2 \in pred\ \rho_2\ 1\ [\![p_2]\!],$$

and so

$$M_2 \in pred\ \rho_2\ 1\ [\![p_1 \lor p_2]\!],$$

and vice versa. For negation, the 'if-and-only-if' wording of the result is essential: if

$$M_1 \in pred\ \rho_1\ 1\ [\![\neg\ p]\!]$$

then

$$M_1 \notin pred \, \rho_1 \, 1 \, \lfloor p \rfloor,$$

so (using the only-if half of the induction hypothesis),

$$M_2 \notin pred \, \rho_2 \, 1 \, \lfloor p \rfloor,$$

that is,

$$M_2 \in pred \, \rho_2 \, 1 \, \lfloor \neg \, p \rfloor,$$

and vice versa. Finally, to deal with quantified predicates, the generalized induction hypothesis is needed to deal with nested scopes: we omit the details here.

Now suppose that the sequent $A \vdash p$ is valid in environment ρ. This is just to say that $M_1 \in pred \, \rho_1 \, 1 \, \lfloor p \rfloor$ for all $M_1 : V_1.models$. Now if we take any model $M_2 : V_2.models$, and define $M_1 = restrict \, V_1.sig \, M_2$, then we have

$$M_1 \in pred \, \rho_1 \, 1 \, \lfloor p \rfloor$$

and so by the result proved above,

$$M_2 \in pred \, \rho_2 \, 1 \, \lfloor p \rfloor,$$

so the sequent $A \wedge B \vdash p$ is valid also.

5.2   Specifying basic types

Throughout the text, we have been using the natural numbers N in giving examples of types, assuming that it was a built-in primitive type of the notation. This section shows that the natural numbers do not have to be built in, because they can be defined axiomatically by a Z specification. Of course, regarding N as built in brings advantages of convenience—for instance, it allows us to use ordinary decimal notation to denote particular natural numbers—but the point is that this adds no power of description to the notation. The specification of N is also an example of the practice of developing a specification in a way that ensures its consistency.

We start by defining a *Peano system* to be a structure consisting of a set X together with a distinguished element *zero* and an injective function *succ* from X into itself. The element *zero* represents 0 within the system, and *succ* represents the successor function. There is an axiom saying that *zero* is not the successor of any other element of X, and an induction principle saying that any subset of X containing *zero* and closed under *succ* is the whole of X. In Z, we make X a generic parameter of a schema, the components of which are *zero* and *succ*:

$$
\begin{array}{|l}
\_PEANO[X]_____ \\
zero : X \\
succ : X \rightarrowtail X \\
\hline
zero \notin \operatorname{ran} succ \\
\forall A : \mathbf{P}\,X \bullet \\
\qquad zero \in A \wedge succ(\!|A|\!) \subseteq A \Rightarrow A = X \\
\end{array}
$$

There are two things to prove about Peano systems. We must first show that at least one such system exists: in Z terms, we must show, for some well-defined term t,

$$\vdash \exists\, PEANO[t].$$

Secondly, we must show that any two Peano systems are isomorphic, so that the structure characterized by the Peano axioms is essentially unique. In Z terms,

$$
\begin{aligned}
&PEANO[X] \wedge PEANO'[Y] \vdash \\
&\quad \exists!\, h : X \rightarrowtail Y \bullet \\
&\qquad h(zero) = zero' \wedge \\
&\qquad (\forall x : X \bullet h(succ(x)) = succ'(h(x))).
\end{aligned}
$$

The first of these facts cannot be proved using just the Z logic, because there is no suitable material for constructing the term t. It can however be proved by a construction in the world of sets, and we can perform even this proof within the Z framework by starting from the world-of-sets specification of section 2.1. If we assume the consistency of this specification—an assumption we might justify by other reasoning independent of Z—then we can use it to help in proving the consistency of other specifications.

A Peano system can be constructed from the infinite set *bigset* in the familiar way, following e.g. (Enderton, 1977). We begin by defining $u : W$ to be the intersection of all inductive subsets of *bigset*, that is, those subsets of *bigset* containing *null* and closed under the operation taking x to $x \sqcup sing(x)$:

$$
\begin{aligned}
u = filter(bigset, \{\, x : W \mid \forall y : W \bullet \\
\quad null \sqsubseteq y \wedge (\forall z : W \bullet z \sqsubseteq y \Rightarrow z \sqcup sing(z) \sqsubseteq y) \Rightarrow x \sqsubseteq y \,\}).
\end{aligned}
$$

It is then easy to show that u is inductive, and that any inductive subset of u is equal to u itself.

This entire construction has taken place inside the 'toy' world of sets, but it can be 'lifted' to the Z level by using the abstraction function *abs*. If we define

$$
\begin{array}{|l}
U : \mathbf{P}\, W \\
zero_0 : W \\
succ_0 : W \twoheadrightarrow W \\
\hline
U = abs(u) \\
zero_0 = null \\
succ_0 = \lambda\, x : U \bullet x \sqcup sing(x).
\end{array}
$$

then these together form a Peano system:

$$\vdash\ PEANO_0[U],$$

and this establishes the required consistency result.

The second fact can be proved entirely within the Z framework. We first use the induction principle of the Peano system to prove a recursion theorem:

$$
\begin{aligned}
PEANO[X];\ &a : Y;\ g : Y \to Y \vdash \\
&\exists!\, h : X \to Y \bullet \\
&\quad h(zero) = a\ \wedge \\
&\quad (\forall\, x : X \bullet h(succ(x)) = g(h(x))),
\end{aligned}
$$

then use this to establish the desired isomorphism.

When these two facts have been established, we can introduce a given set N to model the natural numbers, and fix on a particular Peano system based on N:

$$[N]$$

$$PEANO[N]$$

The use of the given-set name N may seem a little strange. Given sets are more commonly used to denote sets whose particular members are of no interest, and we imagine that the given-set name may have any value at all in a model of the specification. Here the sets which may be used as values of N are rather restricted - they are just the countably infinite sets. But the situation is rather less unusual than it at first appears. Ordinary specifications commonly do place restrictions on the sets which may be used as values of given-set names: an editor, for example, may treat blanks specially, and so its specification might name the blank character:

[*CH*]

blank : *CH*

This immediately restricts the set of characters to be non-empty. To give another example, a filing system may need to store file-names in directories, so may assume that file-names can be encoded in one word of data:

[*DATA, FN*]

encode : $FN \rightarrowtail DATA$

This entails, for example, that if the set *DATA* is finite, then so is the set of possible file-names. There is also an important sense in which we do not care about the particular elements of N, in that all we require is that they behave in an appropriate way with respect to the operations of arithmetic: in concrete terms, we do not care whether numbers are represented in binary or in decimal, so long as addition works properly.

The consistency proof presented above is perhaps atypical, in that it starts from the rather abstruse world-of-sets specification, but consistency proofs along the same lines are useful in everyday specification practice: once we have established, for example, that this specification of the natural numbers is consistent, it can be used in proving the consistency of further specifications. Similar techniques allow the explicit construction of models for the specifications which result from the use of abstract syntax notation. For example, the definition of the binary trees,

$$TREE ::= nil \mid node \, \langle\!\langle \mathbb{N} \times TREE \times TREE \rangle\!\rangle,$$

is equivalent to a specification which introduces a given-set name *TREE* and declares two global constants *nil* and *node* which satisfy axioms similar to those of Peano systems:

$$
\begin{array}{|l}
nil : TREE \\
node : \mathbb{N} \times TREE \times TREE \rightarrowtail TREE \\
\hline
nil \notin \mathrm{ran}\, node \\
\forall S : \mathbb{P}\, TREE \bullet \\
\quad (nil \in S \land node\langle\!|\, \mathbb{N} \times S \times S \,|\!\rangle \subseteq S) \\
\quad\quad \Rightarrow S = TREE
\end{array}
$$

A model for this specification of trees can be constructed using sequences. We say a sequence a is a *prefix* of another sequence b if a copy of a appears at the beginning of b:

$$
\begin{array}{|l}
\hline
\ [X] \\\hline
\ \_ \text{ prefix } \_ : \text{seq } X \leftrightarrow \text{seq } X \\\hline
\ a \text{ prefix } b \Leftrightarrow \\
\qquad \exists\, c : \text{seq } X \bullet b = a \,^\frown c. \\
\hline
\end{array}
$$

A *tree domain* is a finite set of sequences of binary digits with the following property: if it contains some sequence a, then it contains all prefixes of a:

$$TREEDOM \;\hat{=}\; \{\, A : \mathbf{F}(\text{seq}\{0,1\}) \mid$$
$$(\forall\, a, b : \text{seq}\,\{0,1\} \bullet a \text{ prefix } b \wedge b \in A \Rightarrow a \in A)\}$$

The idea is that a tree domain is a set of labels for the nodes of a binary tree, with the root being labelled by the empty sequence $\langle\rangle$ and the left and right descendants of a node labelled a being labelled by $a \,^\frown \langle 0 \rangle$ and $a \,^\frown \langle 1 \rangle$. With these definitions, a tree can be viewed as a function whose domain is a tree domain, and which maps the label of each node to the natural number stored at that node:

$$TREE_0 \;\hat{=}\; \{\, t : \text{seq}\,\{0,1\} \nrightarrow \mathbb{N} \mid \text{dom } t \in TREEDOM \,\}.$$

Now nil_0 is the empty function: the empty set of sequences of binary digits is a tree domain, because it is (vacuously) closed under taking prefixes. If t and u are trees, the tree $cons_0(n, t, u)$ is made up of shifted copies of t and u, with n inserted at the root.

$$
\begin{array}{|l}
\hline
\ nil_0 : TREE \\
\ cons_0 : \mathbb{N} \times TREE \times TREE \to TREE \\
\ \mathit{left}, \mathit{right} : \text{seq}\,\{0,1\} \to \text{seq}\,\{0,1\} \\\hline
\ nil_0 = \varnothing \\
\ cons_0(n, t, u) = \{\langle\rangle \mapsto n\} \cup (t \circ \mathit{left}^{-1}) \cup (u \circ \mathit{right}^{-1}) \\
\ \mathit{left}(a) = \langle 0 \rangle \,^\frown a \\
\ \mathit{right}(a) = \langle 1 \rangle \,^\frown a \\
\hline
\end{array}
$$

The function $cons_0$ is injective, because the three arguments of the composite tree $t = cons_0(n, u, v)$ can be recovered as $n = t(\langle\rangle)$, $u = t \circ \mathit{left}$ and

$v = t \circ right$; nil_0 is not in its range because $cons(n, u, v)$ is always non-empty. Finally, structural induction on trees can be justified by appealing to induction on the size of the domain.

5.3 Specifications and programs

The semantics for Z given in chapter 3 shows how we can regard Z specifications as describing certain structures in set theory. In practice, however, Z specifications are written with the intention of describing not an abstract mathematical structure, but the requirements for a computer program: this is the reason for our interest in specifications in the first place. So what is the relationship between the meaning of specifications as describing set-theoretic structures and their meaning as specifying computer programs? To answer this question, we must add to the bare set-theoretic semantics some extra conventions about the correspondence between specifications and programs.

An *abstract data type* is a structure (S, I, OP, IN, OUT, R) where

- S is a set of *states*,

- I is a subset of S containing *initial states*,

- OP is a set of *operations*, and

- for each operation $p : OP$,

    - IN_p and OUT_p are two sets,

    - $R_p : IN_p \times S \leftrightarrow OUT_p \times S$ is a *meaning relation*.

An abstract data type can be thought of as describing a non-deterministic mechanism with states S. The mechanism is initially in some state taken from I, and is prepared to engage in various operations from OP. When the mechanism is in state $s : S$ and engages in operation $p : OP$, it first accepts an input i drawn from IN_p. If $(i, s) \in \text{dom } R_p$, the activity of the mechanism eventually terminates, leaving it in a state t and producing output o such that $(i, s) \, R_p \, (o, t)$. If $(i, s) \notin \text{dom } R_p$, the subsequent behaviour of the mechanism is not determined: it may produce any output in OUT_p and terminate activity in any state, or its activity may continue forever.

This characterization of abstract data types differs from some definitions in the literature—e.g. (Guttag & Horning, 1978)—in that it allows for partial operations and non-determinacy, but these features have for some time been part of the development method VDM (Jones, 1980, 1986). Recent work in Manchester (Nipkow, 1986) and Oxford (He, Hoare & Sanders, 1986) has extended and generalized the data refinement techniques described in this earlier work. The work of Wirsing and Broy (1982) also extends algebraic specification to cope with partial operations.

Z specifications of appropriate form can be regarded as determining an abstract data type in this sense. Imagine that a model

$$M \in \rho.global.models$$

for the global part of an environment ρ is fixed. The state-space S of the abstract data type is specified by a schema $STATE$ in the Z specification, and is the value of the term $\{ STATE \bullet \theta STATE \}$ in the model M: it is the set of models of $STATE$ which agree with M. The set of initial states I will similarly be specified by a schema $INIT$ which includes $STATE$.

Each operation p is specified by a schema P which includes both $STATE$ and $STATE'$, as well as some components decorated with '?' and '!'. The sets IN_p and OUT_p are the schema products of the types of the components decorated with '?' and '!' respectively, and the meaning relation R_p is such that $(i, s) \; R_p \; (o, t)$ just if there is a model of the schema P extending M which gives these values to the dashed and undashed state components and the input and output components.

This characterization of an abstract data type by a Z specification depends on the choice of a model M for the global part of the specification. If there is just one such model, then the data type is specified unambiguously; but if there is more than one, we say the specification is *loose*, and think of it as specifying not a single abstract data type but a family of abstract data types in the sense defined above, one for each model of the global part.

Loose specifications are encountered in practice for a variety of reasons. The most common reason is the presence of global given-set names, and the choice among the abstract data types in the family amounts to the fixing of these sets. This may be done by the author of the specification with information outside the specification itself: "Let $CHAR$ be the character set of the host computer"; or the choice may be left to the implementor of the specification: "The system must have a set ID of identifiers for users". Looseness is also caused by the presence of incompletely specified global constants, and again, the choice of values may be the responsibility either of the specifier or of the implementor. For example, a specification may depend on an encoding of characters as natural numbers which is not defined exactly in the specification:

$$\begin{array}{|l}
encode : CHAR \rightarrowtail \mathsf{N} \\
\hline
\exists\, n : \mathsf{N} \bullet \mathrm{ran}\ encode = 1 \mathinner{\ldotp\ldotp} n
\end{array}$$

This encoding might be fixed by the choice of computer or by international standard, or might be left to the whim of the programmer implementing the specification.

Loose specifications are useful because they allow the scope of a formal specification to be restricted to a particular area of interest whilst still mentioning objects from outside that area—these objects can be named as loosely specified constants within the specification. They also allow the implementor's freedom to be more precisely described, as the following example shows.

Imagine a box with a single push-button and a display. Every time the button is pressed, a positive number appears in the display, and the sequence of numbers displayed is strictly increasing. We can specify this system using a state containing just the last number displayed:

$$STATE \;\widehat{=}\; [\,last : \mathsf{N}\,]$$

In the initial state, we pretend that the last number displayed was zero:

$$INIT \;\widehat{=}\; [\,STATE \mid last = 0\,]$$

When the button is pressed, a number is displayed which is strictly greater than that displayed last, and the record of the last number displayed is updated:

$$\begin{array}{|l}
\underline{\;BUTTON\;\rule{5cm}{0pt}} \\
STATE \\
STATE' \\
display! : \mathsf{N} \\
\hline
display! > last \\
last' = display!
\end{array}$$

Now we can also specify that each number displayed is three more than the last by replacing the predicate $display! > last$ with $display! = last + 3$: this would be a deterministic specification stronger than the original one, but it would remove all choice from the implementor. By making the specification loose, we can specify that the display should always increase by the same amount but leave the choice of this amount up to the implementor. We introduce a global constant *inc*, which must be strictly positive:

$$\begin{array}{|l}
inc : \mathsf{N} \\
\hline
inc > 0
\end{array}$$

Now we replace the predicate $display! \geq last$ with

$$display! = last + inc,$$

and the result is a specification which is deterministic (in the sense that each data type in its family is deterministic), but which still leaves room for a range of implementations.

5.4   Why non-determinism is needed

If non-deterministic mechanisms are to be specified, it is clear that non-deterministic specifications will be needed. In this section, I give an example to show that they are needed even if only deterministic mechanisms are considered. The example consists of a non-deterministic specification and two deterministic implementations of this specification as Pascal-like programs. One of these satisfies a deterministic strengthening of the original specification, but the other does not satisfy any such strengthening.

5.4.1   *Example: allocating printers*

Imagine a computer installation where a software module is needed to manage allocation of line-printers to jobs. The printers are completely interchangeable, and the module must allocate printers to jobs when requested, whilst ensuring that no printer is ever allocated to more than one job at once. We ignore for present purposes the need to ensure mutual exclusion among the jobs using the printer-allocation module, imagining it to be realized using a 'monitor' (Hoare, 1974). More seriously, we also ignore the possibility of allowing jobs to wait rather than aborting them when no printer is free.

Let *PRINTER* be a set of names for line-printers. The manager must keep track of the set of printers which are free:

$$\begin{array}{|l}
\underline{MANAGER}\underline{\hspace{5cm}} \\
free : \mathsf{P}\ PRINTER \\
\hline
\end{array}$$

$$\Delta MANAGER \;\; \widehat{=} \;\; MANAGER \wedge MANAGER'$$

Allocation involves the selection of a free printer, which is then removed from the pool and returned to the requesting job:

```
┌─ Alloc ──────────────────────────────────────
│ ΔMANAGER
│ lpr! : PRINTER
├──────────────────────────────────────────────
│ lpr! ∈ free
│ free' = free − {lpr!}
└──────────────────────────────────────────────
```

Releasing a printer results in its being returned to the pool:

```
┌─ Release ────────────────────────────────────
│ ΔMANAGER
│ lpr? : PRINTER
├──────────────────────────────────────────────
│ lpr? ∉ free
│ free' = free ∪ {lpr?}
└──────────────────────────────────────────────
```

This specification is non-deterministic because if more than one printer is free, the operation *Alloc* may allocate any one of them.

The pre-condition for *Alloc* is just that the pool of free printers is not empty:

```
┌─ preAlloc ───────────────────────────────────
│ MANAGER
├──────────────────────────────────────────────
│ free ≠ ∅
└──────────────────────────────────────────────
```

The pre-condition for *Release* is that the printer to be released is not free already:

```
┌─ preRelease ─────────────────────────────────
│ MANAGER
│ lpr? : PRINTER
├──────────────────────────────────────────────
│ lpr? ∉ free
└──────────────────────────────────────────────
```

5.4.2 *A first implementation*

A possible implementation of the printer manager identifies printers by small integers; the *Alloc* operation always allocates the free printer with the smallest number. For robustness, an error is reported if an operation is called when its pre-condition is not satisfied.

```
module Manager;
export Printer, Alloc, Release;

    const N = 10;
    type Printer = 1 .. N;
    var free: set of Printer;

    procedure Alloc(var lpr: Printer);
        var k: Printer;
    begin
        if free = [] then
            Error('No printers available');
        k := 1;
        while not (k in free) do k := k + 1;
        lpr := k; free := free - [lpr]
    end (* Alloc *);

    procedure Release(lpr: Printer);
    begin
        if lpr in free then
            Error('Printer already free');
        free := free + [lpr]
    end (* Release *);

begin
    free := [1 .. N]
end (* Manager *).
```

5.4.3 *Strengthening the specification*

The original specification was non-deterministic, but it can be strengthened
to a deterministic specification which is still satisfied by the implementation
above. One way to do this would be to introduce the representation of
printer names as small integers into the specification, and strengthen the
specification of *Alloc* to select the minimum. A less drastic alternative is to
specify only that some fixed function *policy* is used to select the printer to
be allocated, this selection being based on the set of free printers, and being
such that the printer chosen is always free. This gives a loose specification,
but one that is still deterministic.

$$\begin{array}{|l|}
\hline
policy : \mathbf{P}_1 \, PRINTER \rightarrow PRINTER \\
\hline
\forall S : \mathbf{P}_1 \, PRINTER \bullet policy(S) \in S \\
\hline
\end{array}$$

The *Alloc* operation applies this policy:

$$\begin{array}{|l|}
\hline
\_Alloc1 _____ \\
\; Alloc \\
\hline
\; lpr! = policy(free) \\
\hline
\end{array}$$

The specification is deterministic because it requires the printer allocated to be determined as a function of the initial state, so there is only one (output, final state) pair for *Alloc* corresponding to each initial state, but it is loose because it doesn't say which printer in particular is to be allocated.

5.4.4 *Another implementation*

The first implementation satisfied its specification, but it is open to criticism on grounds of performance: because the printers with small numbers will always be allocated in preference to the others, they will wear out more quickly. One way round this is to allocate the printers cyclically, starting the search for a free printer with the next after the one most recently allocated.

```
module Manager;
export Printer, Alloc, Release;

    (* ... *)

    var free: set of Printer;
        last_alloc: Printer;

    procedure Alloc(var lpr: Printer);
        var k: Printer;
    begin
        if free = [] then
            Error('No printers available');
        k := last_alloc mod N + 1;
        while not (k in free) do k := k mod N + 1;
        lpr := k; free := free - [lpr];
        last_alloc := lpr
    end (* Alloc *);
```

```
    procedure Release(lpr: Printer);
    (* ... as before ... *)

begin
    free := [1 .. N];
    last_alloc := N
end (* Manager *).
```

This implementation again satisfies the original specification, but the specification cannot be strengthened to make it deterministic whilst retaining the same abstract state—if several printers are free, the *Alloc* operation may allocate any one of them, and the one it allocates is not determined as a function of the initial (abstract) state. Additional information in the concrete state is used to make the choice, so the implementation is deterministic, even though its strongest specification in terms of the set of free printers is non-deterministic.

REFERENCES

Abrial, J-R. (1984a). Programming as a Mathematical Exercise. In *Mathematical Logic and Programming Languages*, ed. C. A. R. Hoare & J. C. Shepherdson, pp. 113–37. London: Prentice-Hall International.

Abrial, J-R. (1984b). The Mathematical Construction of a Program and its Application to the Construction of Mathematics. *Science of Computer Programming*, 4, 45–86.

Abrial, J-R., Schuman, S. A. & Meyer, B. (1979). Specification Language. In *On the Construction of Programs*, ed. R. M. McKeag & A. M. Macnaghten. Cambridge: Cambridge University Press.

Barringer H., Cheng J. H. & Jones C. B. (1984). A Logic Covering Undefinedness in Program Proofs. *Acta Informatica*, 21, 251–69.

Birkhoff, G. (1967). *Lattice Theory*. American Mathematical Society Colloquium Publications, vol. 25, 3rd. edition.

Bjørner, D. & Jones, C. B. (1982). *Formal Specification and Software Development*. London: Prentice-Hall International.

Blamey, S. R. (1980). *Partial Valued Logic*. D.Phil. thesis. University of Oxford.

Burstall, R. M. & Goguen, J. A. (1980). The Semantics of Clear, a Specification Language. In *Abstract Software Specification*, Lecture Notes in Computer Science, vol. 86, pp. 292–322. Berlin: Springer-Verlag.

Burstall, R. M. & Goguen, J. A. (1981). An Informal Introduction to Specifications using Clear. In *The Correctness Problem in Computer Science*, ed. R. S. Boyer & J. S. Moore, pp. 185–213. London: Academic Press.

Burstall, R. M. & Goguen, J. A. (1982). Algebras, Theories, and Freeness: an Introduction for Computer Scientists. In *Theoretical Foundations of Programming Methodology*, ed. M. Broy & G. Schmidt. Dordrecht, Netherlands: D. Reidel.

Burstall, R. M. & Lampson, B. (1984). A Kernel Language for Abstract Data Types and Modules. In *Semantics of Data Types*, ed. G. Kahn, D. B. MacQueen & G. Plotkin, Lecture Notes in Computer Science, vol. 173, pp. 1–50. Berlin: Springer-Verlag.

Ehrig, H., Fey, W. & Hansen, H. (1983). *ACT ONE: An Algebraic Specification Language with Two Levels of Semantics*. Bericht Nr. 83–03. Institut für Software und Theoretische Informatik, Technische Universität Berlin.

Enderton, H. B. (1977). *Elements of Set Theory*. London: Academic Press.

Goguen, J. A. & Burstall, R. M. (1984). *Institutions: Abstract Model Theory for Program Specification*. University of Edinburgh.

Goguen, J. A. & Tardo, J. J. (1979). An introduction to OBJ, a Language for Writing and Testing Software Specifications. In *Specification of Reliable Software*. New York: Institute of Electrical and Electronics Engineers.

Goguen, J. A., Thatcher, J. W. & Wagner, E. G. (1978). An Initial Algebra Approach to the Specification, Correctness. and Implementation of Abstract Data Types. In *Current Trends in Programming Methodology*, vol. 4, ed. R. T. Yeh, pp. 80–149. Englewood Cliffs, New Jersey: Prentice-Hall.

Guttag, J. V. & Horning, J. J. (1978). The Algebraic Specification of Abstract Data Types. *Acta Informatica*, 10, 27–52.

Hayes, I., editor (1987). *Specification Case Studies*. London: Prentice-Hall International.

He Jifeng, Hoare, C. A. R. & Sanders, J. W. (1986). Data Refinement Refined. In *Proceedings of ESOP'86*, ed. B. Robinet & R. Wilhelm,

Lecture Notes in Computer Science, vol. 213, pp. 187-96. Berlin: Springer-Verlag.

Hoare, C. A. R. (1974). Monitors: an Operating System Structuring Concept. *Communications of the ACM*, 17, 549–57.

Hoare, C. A. R. (1985). *Communicating Sequential Processes*. London: Prentice-Hall International.

Jones, C. B. (1978). The Meta-language: a Reference Manual. In *The Vienna Development Method: the Meta-Language*, ed. D. Bjørner & C. B. Jones, Lecture Notes in Computer Science, vol. 61. Berlin: Springer-Verlag.

Jones, C. B. (1980). *Software Development: a Rigorous Approach*. London: Prentice-Hall International.

Jones, C. B. (1986). *Systematic Software Development using VDM*. London: Prentice-Hall International.

Mac Lane, S. (1971). *Categories for the Working Mathematician*. Berlin: Springer-Verlag.

McCarthy, J. *et al.* (1962). *LISP 1.5 Programmers Manual*. Cambridge, Massachusetts: MIT Press.

Martin-Löf, P. (1984). Constructive Mathematics and Computer Programming. In *Mathematical Logic and Programming Languages*, ed. C. A. R. Hoare & J. C. Shepherdson, pp. 113–37. London: Prentice-Hall International.

Milner, R. G. (1978). A Theory of Type Polymorphism in Programming. *Journal of Computer and System Science*, 17, 348–57.

Morgan, C. C. (1984). *Schemas in Z: a Preliminary Reference Manual*. Programming Research Group, University of Oxford.

Morgan, C. C. & Sufrin, B. A. (1982). Specification of the UNIX Filing System. *IEEE Transactions on Software Engineering*, 10, 128–42.

Nipkow, T. (1986). Nondeterministic Data Types: Models and Implementations. *Acta Informatica*, 22, 629–661.

Plotkin, G. (1981). *A Structural Approach to Operational Semantics*. Report DAIMI FN–19. Computer Science Department, Aarhus University, Denmark.

Reynolds, J. C. (1972). Definitional Interpreters for Higher-Order Programming Languages. In *Proceedings of the 25th ACM National Conference.* New York: Association for Computing Machinery.

Sannella, D. T. (1981). *A New Semantics for Clear.* Technical Report CSR–79–81. Department of Computer Science, University of Edinburgh.

Sannella, D. T. (1982). *Semantics, Implementation, and Pragmatics of Clear, a Program Specification Language.* Ph.D. thesis CST–17–82. Department of Computer Science, University of Edinburgh.

Sannella, D. T. & Tarlecki, A. (1984). Building Specifications in an Arbitrary Institution. In *Semantics of Data Types*, ed. G. Kahn, D. B. MacQueen & G. Plotkin, Lecture Notes in Computer Science, vol. 173, pp. 337–56. Berlin: Springer-Verlag.

Sannella, D. T. & Wirsing, M. (1983). *A Kernel Language for Algebraic Specification and Implementation.* Technical Report CSR–131–83. Department of Computer Science, University of Edinburgh.

Stoy, J. E. (1977). *Denotational Semantics: the Scott-Strachey Approach to Programming Language Theory.* Cambridge, Massachusetts: MIT Press.

Sufrin, B. A. (1983). Formal Specification of a Display-oriented Text Editor. *Science of Computer Programming*, 1, 157–202.

Sufrin, B. A. (1984). *Notes for a Z Handbook: Part I—the Mathematical Language.* Programming Research Group, University of Oxford.

Wirsing, M. & Broy, M. (1982). An Analysis of Semantic Models for Algebraic Specifications. In *Theoretical Foundations of Programming Methodology*, ed. M. Broy & G. Schmidt. Dordrecht, Netherlands: D. Reidel.

Wirth, N. (1977). MODULA: a Language for Modular Multiprogramming. *Software—Practice and Experience*, 7, 3–35.

SUMMARY OF NOTATION

What follows is a brief description of the standard notation, followed by a glossary of those standard Z symbols (the 'mathematical library') which are used in the book. The notation used in giving the denotational semantics is largely 'standard' Z, with the few exceptions described in section 2.4. Parts of this summary are adapted from the 'Z reference card' of Ian Hayes.

Z notation

The Z notation is based on first-order predicate calculus and typed set theory, and the notation used for these parts of the language is very close to that used in ordinary mathematics, with the addition of some special-purpose symbols explained in the glossary below. Most of the formal text in this book consists of definitions of constants. These definitions are given in the form

$$square : \mathbb{N} \to \mathbb{N}$$
$$square(n) = n * n$$

Constants are introduced by declaring them above the horizontal line and giving each of them a type, which for present purposes can be thought of as a set from which the constant is taken. Below the horizontal line are axioms which relate the constants declared above the line with each other and with previously introduced constants; by convention, outermost universal quantifiers may be omitted in these axioms when this causes no ambiguity. The example here introduces a total function *square* from the set of natural numbers to itself, and the value of the function is fixed by an axiom to be the square of its argument.

A Z specification, as well as introducing constants defined by axioms, may start with a number of sets which are assumed given, and which are not further described by the specification — for example, the set of identifiers *IDENT* in section 2.1 is assumed given, because the particular rules about what is an acceptable identifier do not affect the semantics and so are not of interest for present purposes.

A Z feature known as 'schemas' allows a definition of the form explained above to be associated with a name, for example,

$$
\begin{array}{|l}
\hline
\_SQPAIR_____ \\
\quad x, y : \mathbb{N} \\
\hline
\quad y = square(x) \\
\hline
\end{array}
$$

This schema definition does not cause the names x and y to become part of the current context, but instead associates them with the name *SQPAIR*, so that it describes a relationship between x and y which holds just when y is the square of x. Later in the specification, the name *SQPAIR* can be used as an abbreviation for the text inside the box. For example, the predicate

$$\forall\, SQPAIR \bullet y \geq x$$

is equivalent to

$$\forall\, x, y : \mathbb{N} \mid y = square(x) \bullet y \geq x,$$

and the term

$$\{\, SQPAIR \bullet x + y \,\}$$

is equivalent to

$$\{\, x, y : \mathbb{N} \mid y = square(x) \bullet x + y \,\}.$$

Schemas can be defined by extending other schemas: if the name of a previously defined schema is mentioned above the line in a schema definition, its declarations and axioms are thought of as being included among the declarations and axioms of the schema being defined. When two schemas are jointly extended in defining a third, any variables common to both of them are shared in the result, provided that they have the same types.

The term $\{\, SQPAIR \,\}$ denotes a set of 'schema objects' or 'bindings'. Each such object has one component for each variable of the schema, and these are written e.g. $a.x$ and $a.y$; the set $\{\, SQPAIR \,\}$ contains exactly those objects whose components satisfy $y = square(x)$. The curly brackets may be omitted where this is not confusing. Particular schema objects may be written using the μ notation; for example, the object denoted by the μ-term

$$\mu\, SQPAIR \mid x = 4 \wedge y = 16$$

has components 4 and 16. The term $\theta SQPAIR$ denotes an object a whose components $a.x$ and $a.y$ are the values of the variables x and y in the current context.

Z allows schemas to be combined with a variety of operations to give other schemas, and also schemas which have generic parameters, but these facilities are not used in the body of the book, so I shall not describe them here.

Finally, a useful Z feature is 'abstract syntax rules'. These are used in the book to give the abstract syntax of types and of the object language in the denotational semantics. A simple example is the definition of binary trees:

$$TREE ::= nil \mid node\, \langle\!\langle \mathsf{N} \times TREE \times TREE \rangle\!\rangle$$

This introduces two constants *nil* and *node*:

$$
\begin{array}{l}
nil : TREE \\
node : \mathsf{N} \times TREE \times TREE \rightarrowtail TREE \\
\hline
nil \notin \operatorname{ran} node \\
\forall S : \mathsf{P}\, TREE \bullet \\
\quad (nil \in S \wedge node(\!|\mathsf{N} \times S \times S|\!) \subseteq S) \Rightarrow S = TREE
\end{array}
$$

The total function *node* is an injection, and *nil* is not in its range. There is also a structural induction principle, which allows general properties of binary trees to be derived.

Logic

$\neg\, P$	Not P.
$P \wedge Q$	P and Q.
$P \vee Q$	P or Q.
$P \Rightarrow Q$	P implies Q.
$P \Leftrightarrow Q$	P if and only if Q.
$\forall x : T \mid P \bullet Q$	All x of type T satisfying P also satisfy Q.
$\forall x : T \bullet Q$	All x of type T satisfy Q (a special case).
$\exists\, x : T \mid P \bullet Q$	Some x of type T satisfies both P and Q.
$\exists! x : T \mid P \bullet Q$	Exactly one x of type T satisfies both P and Q.

Sets

$x \in S$	x is a member of S.
$S \subseteq T$	S is a subset of T. $\mathrel{\widehat{=}} \forall x : S \bullet x \in T$
$\varnothing$	The empty set.
$\{x_1, \ldots, x_n\}$	The set containing exactly $x_1, \ldots, x_n$.
$\{\, x : T \mid P \,\}$	The set containing those x of type T which satisfy P.
$\{\, x : T \mid P \bullet t \,\}$	The set of values of t for those x of type T satisfying P.
$\mu x : T \mid P$	The unique x of type T which satisfies P.
$\mu x : T \mid P \bullet t$	The value of t for that unique x of type T satisfying P.
$(x_1, \ldots, x_n)$	Ordered n-tuple.
$S_1 \times \cdots \times S_n$	Cartesian product. $\mathrel{\widehat{=}} \{\, x_1 : S_1;\ \ldots;\ x_n : S_n \bullet (x_1, \ldots, x_n) \,\}$
$\mathbf{P}\, S$	The set of all subsets of S.
$\mathbf{F}\, S$	The set of all finite subsets of S.

$S \cap T$	Intersection of S and T. $\widehat{=} \{ x : X \mid x \in S \land x \in T \}$
$S \cup T$	Union of S and T. $\widehat{=} \{ x : X \mid x \in S \lor x \in T \}$
$S \setminus T$	Set difference. $\widehat{=} \{ x : X \mid x \in S \land x \notin T \}$
$\bigcup SS$	Generalized union. $\widehat{=} \{ x : X \mid (\exists S : SS \bullet x \in S) \}$
$\#S$	Size of finite set S.
$\mathbb{N}$	The natural numbers, $\{0, 1, 2, \ldots\}$.
$m \mathbin{..} n$	The range m up to n. $\widehat{=} \{ k : \mathbb{N} \mid m \leq k \land k \leq n \}$

Relations

$X \leftrightarrow Y$	Binary relations between X and Y. $\widehat{=} \mathbb{P}(X \times Y)$
$x \, R \, y$	x and y are related by R. $\widehat{=} (x, y) \in R$
$x \mapsto y$	'Maplet' from x to y. $\widehat{=} (x, y)$
$\mathrm{dom}\, R$	Domain of R. $\widehat{=} \{ x : X \mid (\exists y : Y \bullet x \, R \, y) \}$
$\mathrm{ran}\, R$	Range of R. $\widehat{=} \{ y : Y \mid (\exists x : X \bullet x \, R \, y) \}$
$R_1 \circ R_2$	Composition of relations. $\widehat{=} \{ x : X;\, z : Z \mid (\exists y : Y \bullet x \, R_2 \, y \land y \, R_1 \, z) \}$
R^{-1}	Inverse of R. $\widehat{=} \{ y : Y;\, x : X \mid x \, R \, y \}$
$\mathrm{id}\, S$	Identity relation on S. $\widehat{=} \{ x : S \bullet x \mapsto x \}$

$R(\!(S)\!)$	Relational image. $\hat{=} \{ y : Y \mid (\exists x : S \bullet x\, R\, y) \}$
$S \lhd R$	Domain restriction. $\hat{=} \{ x : X; y : Y \mid x \in S \wedge x\, R\, y \}$
$R \rhd T$	Range restriction. $\hat{=} \{ x : X; y : Y \mid x\, R\, y \wedge y \in T \}$

Functions

$X \nrightarrow Y$	Partial functions from X to Y. $\hat{=} \{ f : X \leftrightarrow Y \mid f \circ f^{-1} \subseteq \operatorname{id} Y \}$
$X \rightarrow Y$	Total functions from X to Y. $\hat{=} \{ f : X \nrightarrow Y \mid \operatorname{dom} f = X \}$
$X \nrightarrow\!\!\!\!\!\rightarrow Y$	Finite partial functions from X to Y. $\hat{=} \{ f : X \nrightarrow Y \mid \operatorname{dom} f \in \mathsf{F}\, X \}$
$X \rightarrowtail\!\!\!\!\!\rightarrow Y$	Partial injections from X to Y. $\hat{=} \{ f : X \nrightarrow Y \mid f^{-1} \in Y \nrightarrow X \}$
$X \rightarrowtail Y$	Total injections from X to Y. $\hat{=} (X \rightarrowtail\!\!\!\!\!\rightarrow Y) \cap (X \rightarrow Y)$
$X \rightarrowtail\!\!\!\!\!\rightarrow Y$	Bijections from X to Y. $\hat{=} \{ f : X \rightarrowtail Y \mid \operatorname{ran} f = Y \}$
$f\, x,\ f(x)$	Function f applied to argument x. Note: $f\, x\, y \;\hat{=}\; (f\, x)\, y$. $\hat{=} \mu\, y : Y \mid x\, f\, y$
$\lambda\, x : T \mid P \bullet t$	Lambda-notation. $\hat{=} \{ x : T \mid P \bullet x \mapsto t \}$
$f \oplus g$	Functional overriding. $\hat{=} ((X \setminus \operatorname{dom} g) \lhd f) \cup g$

Sequences

$\operatorname{seq} X$	Sequences over X. $\hat{=} \{ s : \mathbb{N} \nrightarrow\!\!\!\!\!\rightarrow X \mid \operatorname{dom} s = 1 .. \# s \}$

$\#s$	Length of s (c.f. $\#$ for sets).
$\langle\rangle$	Empty sequence. $\cong \varnothing$
$\langle x_1, \ldots, x_n \rangle$	The sequence containing $x_1, \ldots, x_n$. $\cong \{1 \mapsto x_1, \ldots, n \mapsto x_n\}$
$s \frown t$	Concatenation of s and t.

INDEX OF DEFINITIONS

⊑ 19
⊔ 21
⊑ 21
⊓ 22
⟨ ⟩ 27
[ ] 36
≅ 37
μ 42
◇ 53
:: 60
⇛ 61

abs 25
add_defs 88
add_schema 56
arid 55

basename 55
basis 55
bigset 21
binding 24
blank 53

Carrier 28
combine 43
couple 23
cproduct 24

DECL 50
decl 57
DECOR 53
decorate 53
disjoin 44
dom 127

enrich 56
ENV 54, 87
eval in TMEANING 60
extend 66

filter 22
find 53
fparam in SMEANING 54

gdict in ENV 87
given in SIG 31
global in ENV 54
GMEANING 86
Gmeaning 86
gref 52
gset in STRUCT 33

hide 80
hide_sig 80

id 127

IDENT 52
imply 79
instantiate 76

join 32

LEVEL 52
local in *SMEANING* 54
localname 55
locids 55
lookup 52

map 38
models in *VARIETY* 33

NAME 52
NAMEREF 52
names 28
negate 79
new_givens 82
new_var 58
null 20
null_sig 32

one_level 52

paint 53
pair 21
power 21
PRED 50
pred 71
project 44

ran 127
rename 35
rep 25
restrict 34
retag 73

SCHEMA 49
schema 72
SDES 49
sdes 75

sdict in *ENV* 54
seq 128
SEXP 49
sexp 78
SIG 31
sig in *VARIETY* 33
sing 21
SMEANING 54
SPEC 49
spec 81
sproduct 25
STRUCT 33
Struct 33
subsig 32
subvar 34

Tag 52
tag 52
TERM 50
term 60
TMEANING 60
Tmeaning 63
tsubst 29
tuple 24
TYPE 27
Type 28
type in *SIG* 31
    in *TMEANING* 60

union 20
univ 80

val in *STRUCT* 33
VARIETY 33
vars in *SIG* 31
vref 52

W 19
WORD 53